Birds, Beasts and Flowers

Shearsman Classics, Vol. 12

Other titles in the *Shearsman Classics* series:

Birds, Beasts and Flowers

D.H. Lawrence

Shearsman Books

This edition published in the United Kingdom in 2011 by
Shearsman Books Ltd
58 Velwell Road
Exeter EX4 4LD

ISBN 978-1-84861-157-3

The first British edition of *Birds, Beasts and Flowers* was published by
Martin Secker, London in 1923. An illustrated edition followed in 1930.
The American edition—which excluded the tortoise poems in the
'Reptiles' section—appeared one month prior to the British edition and
was published by Thomas Seltzer, Inc., New York. *Tortoises* had been
published as a separate volume by Seltzer in 1921.

The texts of the poems in this edition follow the first British edition and
take no account of the many later revisions made by Lawrence when
the poems were reprinted in the *Collected Poems* (1928). The texts of the
prefatory prose paragraphs at the head of each section were composed
by Lawrence in 1929, and were first published in the illustrated second
edition of the book, published by the Cresset Press in 1930.

Contents

Introduction

D. H. Lawrence began writing the poems in *Birds, Beasts and Flowers* in 1920 and completed the book in 1923. He wrote many of the poems at Fontana Vecchia, the farmhouse at Taormina, Sicily, which he rented between 1920 and 1922. A number of the poems, including *Tortoises*, originally published as a chapbook, and 'The Evangelistic Beasts', were written at San Gervasio near Florence. 'Elephant' was inspired by the Lawrences visit to Ceylon, en route to Australia, where they spent the summer of 1922 and Lawrence wrote 'Kangaroo'. The poems with a New Mexico setting belong to the beginning of the period at Taos in 1923.

The first poem in the book, 'Pomegranate', begins with confident self-assertiveness:

> You tell me I am wrong.
> Who are you, who is anybody to tell me I am wrong?
> I am not wrong.

This confident "voice" is sustained through much of the book. It is not always as aggressive or argumentative as in this opening, though, from time to time, as in 'Hibiscus and Salvia Flowers', Lawrence's anger carries him away, and he rants. At best, the confidence expresses a sense of release.

Lawrence's life in England during and after the war had been a nightmare. The Lawrences had been evicted from Cornwall on suspicion of spying in 1917; *The Rainbow* had been suppressed; and in 1919 Lawrence had been seriously ill. Hostile or uncomprehending reviews, personal conflicts and differences from the dominant intellectual sets added to his sense of embittered isolation. Even more important was the fact that since the war, and largely as a result of the war, Lawrence had been thinking apocalyptically. He felt that not only his society but European civilization, and even the white races in America, were doomed. The release expressed in the poems set in Italy was thus only in part a response to Mediterranean warmth and natural abundance after dreary post-war England. It also reflected what in 'Almond Blossom' he called 'the ancient southern earth' where a more vital, instinctive spirit survived.

This is only part of the story, however. For in Italy in 1920–22 modern politics were very much alive, with Socialists, and Anarchists, and Bolsheviks struggling with Fascists for power. And Lawrence loathed them all. More particularly, he hated mass movements, any grouping that worked against individual distinction. He was hostile to Democracy with its claim of equality among human beings. An idea of leadership based upon individual distinction—a kind of *natural* aristocracy—marks Lawrence's treatment of all beings, not just men. The emphasis is upon the male, for Lawrence's attitude towards woman suggests his fear of female power. The marvellously sensuous poems, such as 'Pomegranate', 'Peach and 'Figs', justly famous for their celebration of female sexuality, are also a man's way of exposing its mysteries to the male gaze, and therefore making it less threatening. Aggression, based upon fear of the female, appears more troublingly in 'Bibbles', with its portrayal of the dog as "you miserable little bitch of love-tricks".

As a poetry of encounter between the poet and the natural world *Birds, Beasts and Flowers* is wonderful. It is Lawrence's supreme achievement of the gift for sensitive relationship with nature's vitality and otherness that he had shown from the beginning, in *The White Peacock*. Before dwelling on this, however, it is necessary to record that the book is much else as well.

In the period that he was writing the poems, Lawrence was remaking himself as a thinker, and the poems were part of the process. He was working not only as a novelist and story writer, but also, in *Psychology and the Unconscious* and *Fantasia of the Unconscious*, on an original psychology, hostile to Freudianism. It is futile to make a distinction between Lawrence's psychology and philosophy, or to keep his poetry separate from his literary criticism. In *Studies in Classic American Literature*, which he had begun earlier and resumed in these years, he was exploring psychological and philosophical ideas that he was also working on in the poems.

Birds, Beasts and Flowers concludes with poems set in New Mexico, but Lawrence's thinking about America preceded the book, and also colours much of it. In *Studies in Classic American Literature* he remarked: "I think this wild and noble America is the thing that I have pined for most ever since I read Fenimore Cooper, as a boy". Characteristically, the attraction was to the idea of a more primitive world. He had made several unsuccessful attempts to go to America before 1923, but his thinking about America had become a matter of repulsion as well as attraction. As he felt Europe was doomed, so he felt

America shared in the same fate, but perhaps with a hope of rebirth. In 'The Evening Land' he addresses America, asking: "Shall I come to you, the open tomb of my race?". He is terrified of: "The winding-sheet of your self-less ideal love./Boundless love/Like a poison gas."

Walt Whitman was the great liberating force for Lawrence as a poet. The influence can be seen, in *Birds, Beasts and Flowers*, in the flexible long lines, the repetition with variation of images and phrases, the questions and statements, and the sustained, inventive thinking with symbols and metaphors. It is everywhere in the release of thought and feeling, which, being personal, allows Lawrence's whole being freedom of expression. Lawrence is like Whitman in his *process* of poetic thinking. His conclusions, however, differ from Whitman's, since he is opposed to "self-less ideal love". As he claims in *Studies in Classic American Literature*, "Love, and Merging, brought Whitman to the Edge of Death! Death! Death!".

Lawrence's thinking in the years during and after the war was strongly influenced by his reading of the pre-Socratic philosophers. Ironically, it was Bertrand Russell who lent him a copy of John Burnet's *Early Greek Philosophy*, which influenced the development of his thought in opposition to Russell's rationalism and belief in Democracy—opposition expressed forcefully in *Birds, Beasts and Flowers*. In July 1915 he wrote to Russell: "I have been wrong, much too Christian, in my philosophy. These early Greeks have clarified my soul. I must drop all about God". He proceeded to invoke Herakleitos in support of his belief in the Ruler: "There must be an aristocracy of people who have wisdom, and there must be a Ruler: a Kaiser: no President and democracies".

Lawrence does not "drop all about God" in the poems. While he invokes pagan myths, the dominant source of his symbols is the Bible. He intensifies his transformation of the Christian story into the terms of his philosophy of life, which owes a special debt to Herakleitos and Empedokles among the ancient cosmologists. Lawrence draws upon Einstein's new physics for his world picture, but he draws more upon the cosmologists' ideas of elements and forces, upon a sense of the world in the making, prior to modern categories and concepts. Above all, he opposes "being" to "knowing".

Mental consciousness resulting in both rationalism and sexual self-awareness is a special target of Lawrence's anger. In *Psychoanalysis and the Unconscious* he ascribes the Fall to Adam and Eve's awareness "that they could deliberately enter upon and enjoy and even provoke sexual activity in themselves". Eve in particular was to blame. Thus, in 'Figs':

> When Eve once knew *in her mind* that she was naked
> She quickly sewed fig-leaves, and sewed the same for the man.
> She'd been naked all her days before,
> But till then, till that apple of knowledge, she hadn't had the
>   fact on her mind.

In a symbolism that is sometimes covert Lawrence opposes the Tree of Life to the Tree of the Knowledge of Good and Evil.

In terms of the Christian plan of salvation, the latter stands, of course, behind the Cross. This is the symbol identified with the ideal of "saviourism", which Lawrence rejects. Some of the most powerful poetry in the book arises from his engagement with this theme, and his transformation of this symbolism. In 'Almond Blossom', for example, he substitutes the flowering tree for the Cross:

> Sweating his drops of blood through the long-nighted
>   Gethsemane
> Into blossom, into pride, into honey-triumph, into most
>   exquisite splendour.
> Oh, give me the tree of life in blossom
> And the Cross sprouting its superb and fearless flowers!

The religious and political themes are closely allied. Lawrence's politics, in fact, can only be understood in terms of his religious thinking. The poems are both expressions of a powerful individuality, and affirmations of what in 'Hibiscus and Salvia Flowers' he calls "passionate disquality of men", in opposition to "foul equality". Lawrence, however, knows the cost of individuality. The Tortoise poems, in particular, explore sex as the painful condition—"the long crucifixion of desire"—that prevents singleness of being. Lawrence quotes Heraldeitos, acknowledging the truth of his words:

> Homer was wrong in saying, "Would that strife might pass
> away from among gods and men!" He did not see that he was
> praying for the destruction of the universe; for, if his prayer

were heard, all things would pass away—for in the tension of opposites all things have their being—

"Divided into passionate duality" ('Lui et Elle'), man cannot be single, alone in the universe.

> Sex, which breaks us into voice, sets us calling across the
>   deeps, calling, calling for the complement,
> Singing, and calling, and singing again, being answered,
>   having found.

> Torn, to become whole again, after long seeking for what
>   is lost,
> The same cry from the tortoise as from Christ, the Osiris-
>   cry of abandonment,
> That which is whole, torn asunder,
> That which is in part, finding its whole again throughout
>   the universe. ('Tortoise Shout')

As these magnificent lines imply, duality, the "struggle of opposites", is the cause of "singing", of poetry. And Lawrence is "torn": he expresses resistance to the very condition on which life depends, and a strong desire to be single. This takes the form of hostility towards the woman as a sexual being. The strangest poem in the collection, 'Spirits Summoned West', seems to express desire for an impossible ideal beyond sex, for the mother as virgin.

The most succinct summary of Lawrence's thought at this period occurs in *Studies in Classic American Literature*:

> KNOWING and BEING are opposite, antagonistic states. The more you know, exactly, the less you *are*. The more you *are*, in being, the less you know.
>   This is the great cross of man, his dualism. The blood-self, and the nerve-brain self.

Lawrence's desire to escape from KNOWING to BEING finds powerful expression in *Birds, Beasts and Flowers*. It appears in his primitivism—in the presence of the Etruscan "secret" in the trees in 'Cypresses', for example; and in his remarkable imagination, in

'Grapes', of the world "long ago", "before eyes saw too much". Then, he imagines "all in naked communion communicating as now our/ clothed vision can never communicate".

But he cannot unknow; he cannot not see. It is only by knowing and seeing that he can approach an opposite condition, life as "the blood-self" apprehends it. In 'Snake', meanly throwing a log at the snake which has preceded him at "my water-trough", he despises "the voices of my accursed human education". But those voices are voices within the poems, and Lawrence's quarrel with them is partly what makes the poems. It is a quarrel within himself, between KNOWING and BEING.

The quarrel can be seen in his use of language. In *Women in Love* Gudrun is condemned for her anthropomorphism, for her fanciful reduction of other creatures to images, products of her clever aestheticism. It is a tendency Lawrence himself has, as his images show. There are many examples in *Birds, Beasts and Flowers*; his description of the She-Goat as "Like a belle at her window" is one. At his best, however, he recognises his knowingness, and rejects it. In 'Fish' he describes "A slim young pike . . ./Slouching along away below, half out of sight,/Like a lout on an obscure pavement". The image is doubly offensive: to the "lout", with the jeering tone Lawrence tended to adopt towards "common" people, and to the fish. As far as the fish is concerned, he rebukes himself:

I had made a mistake, I didn't know him,
This grey, monotonous soul in the water,
    This intense individual in shadow,
    Fish-alive.

    I didn't know his God,
    I didn't know his God.

    Which is perhaps the last admission that life has to wring
        out of us.

Earlier in the poem he has invoked the fish with "Your life a sluice of sensation along your sides". It is one of those marvellous moments, caught in an image or a phrase, which recur throughout *Birds, Beasts and Flowers*. 'On a day of Sicilian July, with Etna smoking' is another example of words once heard, never forgotten. It is an art that characterises whole poems, as well as occurring in phrases, in images, when Lawrence comes to the human "pale", and records a magical awareness of non-human modes of being. With its apocalyptic political vision, and its original psychology, the book includes much more than this sensitivity to nature. It is for this, however, that it is surely most memorable. Altogether *Birds, Beasts and Flowers* is one of the greatest books by an English poet in the twentieth century. Of Melville's achievement in *Moby Dick*, Lawrence says, when he "gives us his sheer apprehension of the world, then he is wonderful, his book commands a stillness in the soul, an awe". This is what Lawrence himself achieves in *Birds, Beasts and Flowers.*

BIRDS, BEASTS AND FLOWERS

Fruits

√ "For fruits are all of them female, in them lies the seed. And so when they break and show the seed, then We look into the womb and see its secrets. So it is that the pomegranate is the apple of love to the Arab, and the fig has been a catch-word for the female fissure for ages. I don't care a fig for it! men say. But why a fig? The apple of Eden, even, Was Eve's fruit. To her it belonged, and she offered lit to the man. Even the apples of knowledge are Eve's fruit, the Woman's. But the apples of life the dragon guards, and no woman gives them . . ."

"No sin is it to drink as much as a man can take and get home without a servant's help, so he be not stricken in years."

Pomegranate

You tell me I am wrong.
Who are you, who is anybody to tell me I am wrong?
I am not wrong.

In Syracuse, rock left bare by the viciousness of Greek women,
No doubt you have forgotten the pomegranate-trees in flower,
Oh so rcd, and such a lot of them.

Whereas at Venice
Abhorrent, green, slippery city
Whose Doges were old, and had ancient eyes,
In the dense foliage of the inner garden
Pomegranates like bright green stone,
And barbed, barbed with a crown.
Oh, crown of spiked green metal
Actually growing!

Now in Tuscany,
Pomegranates to warm, your hands at;
And crowns, kingly, generous, tilting crowns
Over the left eyebrow.

And, if you dare, the fissure!

Do you mean to tell me you will see no fissure?
Do you prefer to look on the plain side?
For all that, the setting suns are open.
The end cracks open with the beginning:
Rosy, tender, glittering within the fissure.

Do you mean to tell me there should be no fissure?
No glittering, compact drops of dawn?
Do you mean it is wrong, the gold-filmed skin, integument, shown
        ruptured?

For my part, I prefer my heart to be broken.
It is so lovely, dawn-kaleidoscopic within the crack.

San Gervasio in Tuscany

19

Peach

Would you like to throw a stone at me?
Here, take all that's left of my peach.

Blood-red, deep;
Heaven knows how it came to pass.
Somebody's pound of flesh rendered up.

Wrinkled with secrets?
And hard with the intention to keep them.

Why, from silvery peach-bloom,
From that shallow-silvery wine-glass on a short stem
This rolling, dropping, heavy globule?

I am thinking, of course, of the peach before I ate it.

Why so velvety, why so voluptuous heavy?
Why hanging with such inordinate weight?
Why so indented?

Why the groove?
Why the lovely, bivalve roundnesses?
Why the ripple down the sphere?
Why the suggestion of incision?

Why was not my peach round and finished like a billiard ball?
It would have been if man had made it.
Though I've eaten it now.

But it wasn't round and finished like a billiard ball.
And because I say so, you would like to throw something at me.

Here, you can have my peach stone.

San Gervasio

20

Medlars and Sorb-Apples

I love you, rotten,
Delicious rottenness.

I love to suck you out from your skins
So brown and soft and coming suave,
So morbid, as the Italians say.

What a rare, powerful, reminiscent flavour
Comes out of your falling through the stages of decay:
Stream within stream.

Something of the same flavour as Syracusan muscat wine
Or vulgar Marsala.

Though even the word Marsala will smack of preciosity
Soon in the pussyfoot West.

What is it?
What is it, in the grape turning raisin,
In the medlar, in the sorb-apple,
Wineskins of brown morbidity,
Autumnal excrementa;
What is it that reminds us of white gods?

Gods nude as blanched nut-kernels,
Strangely, half-sinisterly flesh-fragrant
As if with sweat,
And drenched with mystery.

Sorb-apples, medlars with dead crowns.

I say, wonderful are the hellish experiences
Orphic, delicate
Dionysos of the Underworld.

A kiss, and a vivid spasm of farewell, a moment's orgasm of rupture,
Then along the damp road alone, till the next turning.

And there, a new partner, a new parting, a new unfusing into twain,
A new gasp of further isolation,
A new intoxication of loneliness, among decaying, frost-cold leaves.

Going down the strange lanes of hell, more and more intensely alone,
The fibres of the heart parting one after the other
And yet the soul continuing, naked-footed, ever more vividly embodied
Like a flame blown whiter and whiter
In a deeper and deeper darkness
Ever more exquisite, distilled in separation.

So, in the strange retorts of medlars and sorb-apples
The distilled essence of hell.
The exquisite odour of leave-taking.
    Jamque vale!
Orpheus, and the winding, leaf-clogged, silent lanes of hell.

Each soul departing with its own isolation,
Strangest of all strange companions,
And best.

Medlars, sorb-apples
More than sweet
Flux of autumn
Sucked out of your empty bladders
And sipped down, perhaps, with a sip of Marsala
So that the rambling, sky-dropped grape can add its music to yours,
Orphic farewell, and farewell, and farewell
And the *ego sum* of Dionysos
The *sono io* of perfect drunkenness
Intoxication of final loneliness.

San Gervasio.

Figs

The proper way to eat a fig, in society,
Is to split it in four, holding it by the stump,
And open it, so that it is a glittering, rosy, moist, honied, heavy-
        petalled four-petalled flower.

Then you throw away the skin
Which is just like a four-sepalled calyx,
After you have taken off the blossom with your lips.

But the vulgar way
Is just to put your mouth to the crack, and take out the flesh in one bite.

Every fruit has its secret.

The fig is a very secretive fruit.
As you see it standing growing, you feel at once it is symbolic:
And it seems male.
But when you come to know it better, you agree with the Romans,
        it is female.

The Italians vulgarly say, it stands for the female part; the fig-fruit:
The fissure, the yoni,
The wonderful moist conductivity towards the centre.

Involved,
Inturned,
The flowering all inward and womb-fibrilled;
And but one orifice.

The fig, the horse-shoe, the squash-blossom.
Symbols.

There was a flower that flowered inward, womb-ward;
Now there is a fruit like a ripe womb.

It was always a secret.
That's how it should be, the female should always be secret.

There never was any standing aloft and unfolded on a bough
Like other flowers, in a revelation of petals;
Silver-pink peach, Venetian green glass of medlars and sorb-apples,
Shallow wine-cups on short, bulging stems
Openly pledging heaven:
Here's to the thorn in flower! Here is to Utterance!
The brave, adventurous rosaceae.

Folded upon itself, and secret unutterable,
And milky-sapped, sap that curdles milk and makes *ricotta*,
Sap that smells strange on your fingers, that even goats won't taste it;
Folded upon itself, enclosed like any Mohammedan woman,
Its nakedness all within-walls, its flowering forever unseen,
One small way of access only, and this close-curtained from the light;
Fig, fruit of the female mystery, covert and inward,
Mediterranean fruit, with your covert nakedness,
Where everything happens invisible, flowering and fertilisation, and
   fruiting
In the inwardness of your you, that eye will never see
Till it's finished, and you're over-ripe, and you burst to give up your
   ghost.

Till the drop of ripeness exudes,
And the year is over.

And then the fig has kept her secret long enough.
So it explodes, and you see through the fissure the scarlet.
And the fig is finished, the year is over.

That's how the fig dies, showing her crimson through the purple slit
Like a wound, the exposure of her secret, on the open day.
Like a prostitute, the bursten fig, making a show of her secret.

That's how women die too.

The year is fallen over-ripe,
The year of our women.
The year of our women is fallen over-ripe.
The secret is laid bare.

And rottenness soon sets in.
The year of our women is fallen over-ripe.

When Eve once knew *in her mind* that she was naked
She quickly sewed fig-leaves, and sewed the same for the man.
She'd been naked all her days before,
But till then, till that apple of knowledge, she hadn't had the fact on
      her mind.

She got the fact on her mind, and quickly sewed fig-leaves.
And women have been sewing ever since.
But now they stitch to adorn the bursten fig, not to cover it.
They have their nakedness more than ever on their mind,
And they won't let us forget it.

Now, the secret
Becomes an affirmation through moist, scarlet lips
That laugh at the Lord's indignation.

What then, good Lord! cry the women.
We have kept our secret long enough.
We are a ripe fig.
Let us burst into affirmation.

They forget, ripe figs won't keep.
Ripe figs won't keep.

Honey-white figs of the north, black figs with scarlet inside, of the
      south.
Ripe figs won't keep, won't keep in any clime.
What then, when women the world over have all bursten into
      affirmation?
And bursten figs won't keep."

San Gervasio

Grapes

So many fruits come from roses
From the rose of all roses
From the unfolded rose
Rose of all the world.

Admit that apples and strawberries and peaches and pears and
        blackberries
Are all Rosaceae,
Issue of the explicit rose,
The open-countenanced, skyward-smiling rose.

What then of the vine?
Oh, what of the tendrilled vine?

Ours is the universe of the unfolded rose,
The explicit,
The candid revelation.

But long ago, oh, long ago
Before the rose began to simper supreme,
Before the rose of all roses, rose of all the world, was even in bud.
Before the glaciers were gathered up in a bunch out of the unsettled
        seas and winds,
Or else before they had been let down again, in Noah's flood,
There was another world, a dusky, flowerless, tendrilled world
And creatures webbed and marshy,
And on the margin, men soft-footed and pristine,
Still, and sensitive, and active,
Audile, tactile sensitiveness as of a tendril which orientates and
        reaches out,
Reaching out and grasping by an instinct more delicate than the
        moon's as she feels for the tides.

Of which world, the vine was the invisible rose,
Before petals spread, before colour made its disturbance, before eyes
        saw too much.

In a green, muddy, web-foot, unutterably songless world
The vine was rose of all roses.

There were no poppies or carnations,
Hardly a greenish lily, watery faint.
Green, dim, invisible flourishing of vines
Royally gesticulate.

Look now even now, how it keeps its power of invisibility!
Look how black, how blue-black, how globed in Egyptian darkness
Dropping among his leaves, hangs the dark grape!
See him there, the swart, so palpably invisible:
Whom shall we ask about him?

The negro might know a little.
When the vine was rose, Gods were dark-skinned.
Bacchus is a dream's dream.
Once God was all negroid, as now he is fair.
But it's so long ago, the ancient Bushman has forgotten more utterly
          than we, who have never known.

For we are on the brink of re-remembrance.
Which, I suppose, is why America has gone dry.
Our pale day is sinking into twilight,
And if we sip the wine, we find dreams coming upon us
Out of the imminent night.
Nay, we find ourselves crossing the fern-scented frontiers
Of the world before the floods, where man was dark and evasive
And the tiny vine-flower rose of all roses, perfumed,
And all in naked communion communicating as now our clothed
          vision can never communicate.
Vistas, down dark avenues
As we sip the wine.

The grape is swart, the avenues dusky and tendrilled, subtly prehensile,
But we, as we start awake, clutch at our vistas democratic, boulevards,
          tram-cars, policemen.
Give us our own back
Let us go to the soda-fountain, to get sober.

Soberness, sobriety.
It is like the agonised perverseness of a child heavy with sleep, yet
          fighting, fighting to keep awake;
Soberness, sobriety, with heavy eyes propped open.

Dusky are the avenues of wine,
And we must cross the frontiers, though we will not,
Of the lost, fern-scented world:
Take the fern-seed on our lips,
Close the eyes, and go
Down the tendrilled avenues of wine and the otherworld.

San Gervasio

The Revolutionary

Look at them standing there in authority
The pale-faces,
As if it could have any effect any more.

Pale-face authority,
Caryatids,
Pillars of white bronze standing rigid, lest the skies fall.

What a job they've got to keep it up.
Their poor, idealist foreheads naked capitals
To the entablature of clouded heaven.

When the skies are going to fall, fall they will
In a great chute and rush of debacle downwards.

Oh and I wish the high and super-gothic heavens would come down
        now,
The heavens above, that we yearn to and aspire to.

I do not yearn, nor aspire, for I am a blind Samson.
And what is daylight to me that I should look skyward?
Only I grope among you, pale-faces, caryatids, as among a forest of
        pillars that hold up the dome of high ideal heaven
Which is my prison,
And all these human pillars of loftiness, going stiff, metallic-stunned
        with the weight of their responsibility
I stumble against them.
Stumbling-blocks, painful ones.

To keep on holding up this ideal civilisation
Must be excruciating: unless you stiffen into metal, when it is easier
        to stand stock rigid than to move.

This is why I tug at them, individually, with my arm round their waist
The human pillars.
They are not stronger than I am, blind Samson.
The house sways.

I shall be so glad when it comes down.
I am so tired of the limitations of their Infinite.
I am so sick of the pretensions of the Spirit.
I am so weary of pale-face importance.

Am I not blind, at the round-turning mill?
Then why should I fear their pale faces?
Or love the effulgence of their holy light,
The sun of their righteousness?

To me, all faces are dark,
All lips are dusky and valved.

Save your lips, O pale-faces,
Which are slips of metal,
Like slits in an automatic-machine, you columns of give-and-take.

To me, the earth rolls ponderously, superbly
Coming my way without forethought or afterthought.
To me, men's footfalls fall with a dull, soft rumble, ominous and lovely,
Coming my way.

But not your foot-falls, pale-faces,
They are a clicketing of bits of disjointed metal
Working in motion.

To me, men are palpable, invisible nearnesses in the dark
Sending out magnetic vibrations of warning, pitch-dark throbs of
        invitation.

But you, pale-faces,
You are painful, harsh-surfaced pillars that give off nothing except
        rigidity,
And I jut against you if I try to move, for you are everywhere, and I
        am blind.
Sightless among all your visuality.
You staring caryatids.

See if I don't bring you down, and all your high opinion
And all your ponderous roofed-in erection of right and wrong
Your particular heavens,
With a smash.

See if your skies aren't falling!
And my head, at least, is thick enough to stand it, the smash.

See if I don't move under a dark and nude, vast heaven
When your world is in ruins, under your fallen skies.
Caryatids, pale-faces.
See if I am not Lord of the dark and moving hosts
Before I die.

Florence

The Evening Land

Oh, America,
The sun sets in you.
Are you the grave of our day?

Shall I come to you, the open tomb of my race?

I would come, if I felt my hour had struck.
I would rather you came to me.

For that matter
Mahomet never went to any mountain
Save it had first approached him and cajoled his soul.

You have cajoled the souls of millions of us
America,
Why won't you cajole my soul?
I wish you would.

I confess I am afraid of you.

The catastrophe of your exaggerate love,
You who never find yourself in love
But only lose yourself further, decomposing.

You who never recover from out of the orgasm of loving
Your pristine, isolate integrity, lost aeons ago.
Your singleness within the universe.

You who in loving break down
And break further and further down
Your bounds of isolation,
But who never rise, resurrected, from this grave of mingling,
In a new proud singleness, America.

Your more-than-European idealism,
Like a be-aureoled bleached skeleton hovering
Its cage-ribs in the social heaven, beneficent.

And then your single resurrection
Into machine-uprisen perfect man.

Even the winged skeleton of your bleached ideal
Is not so frightening as that clean smooth
Automaton of your uprisen self,
Machine American.

Do you wonder that I am afraid to come
And answer the first machine-cut question from the lips of your
        iron men?
Put the first cents into metallic fingers of your officers
And sit beside the steel-straight arms of your fair women
American?

This may be a withering tree, this Europe,
But here, even a customs-official is still vulnerable.

I am so terrified, America,
Of the iron click of your human contact.
And after this
The winding-sheet of your self-less ideal love.
Boundless love
Like a poison gas.

Does no one realise that love should be intense, individual,
Not boundless.
This boundless love is like the bad smell
Of something gone wrong in the middle.
All this philanthropy and benevolence on other people's behalf
Just a bad smell.

Yet, America,
Your elvishness,
Your New England uncanniness,
Your western brutal faery quality.

My soul is half-cajoled, half-cajoled.

Something in you which carries me beyond
Yankee, Yankee,
What we call human.
Carries me where I want to be carried . . .
Or don't I?

What does it matter
What we call human, and what we don't call human?
The rose would smell as sweet.
And to be limited by a mere word is to be less than a hopping flea,
          which hops over such an obstruction at first jump.

Your horrible, skeleton, aureoled ideal,
Your weird bright motor-productive mechanism,
Two spectres.

But moreover
A dark, unfathomed will, that is not un-Jewish;
A set, stoic endurance, non-European;
An ultimate desperateness, un-African;
A deliberate generosity, non-Oriental.

The strange, unaccustomed geste of your demonish New World nature
Glimpsed now and then.

Nobody knows you.
You don't know yourself.
And I, who am half in love with you.
What am I in love with?
My own imaginings?

Say it is not so.

Say, through the branches
America, America
Of all your machines,
Say, in the deep sockets of your idealistic skull,
Dark, aboriginal eyes
Stoic, able to wait through ages
Glancing.

Say, in the sound of all your machines
And white words, white-wash American,
Deep pulsing of a strange heart
New throb, like a stirring under the false dawn that precedes the real.

Nascent American
Demonish, lurking among the undergrowth
Of many-stemmed machines and chimneys that smoke like pine-trees.

Dark, elvish,
Modern, unissued, uncanny America,
Your nascent demon people
Lurking among the deeps of your industrial thicket
Allure me till I am beside myself,
A nympholepht.

"These States!" as Whitman said,
Whatever he meant.

Baden-Baden

Peace

Peace is written on the doorstep
In lava.

Peace, black peace congealed.
My heart will know no peace
Till the hill bursts.

Brilliant, intolerable lava
Brilliant as a powerful burning-glass
Walking like a royal snake down the mountain towards the sea.

Forests, cities, bridges
Gone again in the bright trail of lava.
Naxos thousands of feet below the olive-roots,
And now the olive leaves thousands of feet below the lava fire.

Peace congealed in black lava on the doorstep.
Within, white-hot lava, never at peace
Till it burst forth blinding, withering the earth;
To set again into rock
Grey-black rock.

Call it Peace?

Taormina

TREES

"It is said, a disease has attacked the cypress trees of Italy, and they are all dying.

Now even the shadow of the lost secret is vanishing from earth."
"Empedokles says trees were the first living creatures to grow up out of the earth, before the sun was spread out and before day and night were distinguished; from the symmetry of their mixture of fire and water, they contain the proportion of male and female; they grow, rising up owing to the heat which is in the earth, so that they are parts of the earth just as embryos are parts of the uterus. Fruits are excretions of the water and fire in plants."

Cypresses

Tuscan cypresses,
What is it?

Folded in like a dark thought
For which the language is lost,
Tuscan cypresses,
Is there a great secret?
Are our words no good?

The undeliverable secret,
Dead with a dead race and a dead speech, and yet
Darkly monumental in you,
Etruscan cypresses.

Ah, how I admire your fidelity,
Dark cypresses!

Is it the secret of the long-nosed Etruscans?
The long-nosed, sensitive-footed, subtly-smiling Etruscans,
Who made so little noise outside the cypress groves?

Among the sinuous, flame-tall cypresses
That swayed their length of darkness all around
Etruscan-dusky, wavering men of old Etruria:
Naked except for fanciful long shoes,
Going with insidious, half-smiling quietness
And some of Africa's imperturbable sang-froid
About a forgotten business.

What business, then?
Nay, tongues are dead, and words are hollow as hollow seed-pods,
Having shed their sound and finished all their echoing
Etruscan syllables,
That had the telling.

Yet more I see you darkly concentrate,
Tuscan cypresses,

On one old thought:
On one old slim imperishable thought, while you remain
Etruscan cypresses;
Dusky, slim marrow-thought of slender, flickering men of Etruria,
Whom Rome called vicious.

Vicious, dark cypresses:
Vicious, you supple, brooding, softly-swaying pillars of dark flame.
Monumental to a dead, dead race
Embalmed in you!

Were they then vicious, the slender, tender-footed,
Long-nosed men of Etruria?
Or was their way only evasive and different, dark, like cypress-trees
        in a wind?

They are dead, with all their vices,
And all that is left
Is the shadowy monomania of some cypresses
And tombs.

The smile, the subtle Etruscan smile still lurking
Within the tombs,
Etruscan cypresses.
He laughs longest who laughs last;
Nay, Leonardo only bungled the pure Etruscan smile.

What would I not give
To bring back the rare and orchid-like
Evil-yclept Etruscan?

For as to the evil
We have only Roman word for it,
Which I, being a little weary of Roman virtue,
Don't hang much weight on.

For oh, I know, in the dust where we have buried
The silenced races and all their abominations,
We have buried so much of the delicate magic of life.

There in the deeps
That churn the frankincense and ooze the myrrh,
Cypress shadowy,
Such an aroma of lost human life!

They say the fit survive,
But I invoke the spirits of the lost.
Those that have not survived, the darkly lost,
To bring their meaning back into life again,
Which they have taken away
And wrapt inviolable in soft cypress-trees,
Etruscan cypresses.

Evil, what is evil?
There is only one evil, to deny life
As Rome denied Etruria
And mechanical America Montezuma still.

Fiesole

Bare Fig-Trees

Fig-trees, weird fig-trees
Made of thick smooth silver,
Made of sweet, untarnished silver in the sea-southern air—
I say untarnished, but I mean opaque—
Thick, smooth-fleshed silver, dull only as human limbs are dull
With the life-lustre,
Nude with the dim light of full, healthy life
That is always half-dark,
And suave like passion-flower petals,
Like passion-flowers,
With the half-secret gleam of a passion-flower hanging from the rock,
Great, complicated, nude fig-tree, stemless flower-mesh,
Flowerily naked in flesh, and giving off hues of life.

Rather like an octopus, but strange and sweet-myriad-limbed octopus;
Like a nude, like a rock-living, sweet-fleshed sea-anemone,
Flourishing from the rock in a mysterious arrogance.

Let me sit down beneath the many-branching candelabrum
That lives upon this rock
And laugh at Time, and laugh at dull Eternity,
And make a joke of stale Infinity,
Within the flesh-scent of this wicked tree,
That has kept so many secrets up its sleeve,
And has been laughing through so many ages
At man and his uncomfortablenesses,
And his attempt to assure himself that what is so is not so,
Up its sleeve.

Let me sit down beneath this many-branching candelabrum,
The Jewish seven-branched, tallow-stinking candlestick kicked over
        the cliff
And all its tallow righteousness got rid of,
And let me notice it behave itself.

And watch it putting forth each time to heaven,
Each time straight to heaven,

With marvellous naked assurance each single twig,
Each one setting off straight to the sky
As if it were the leader, the main-stem, the forerunner,
Intent to hold the candle of the sun upon its socket-tip.
It alone.

Every young twig
No sooner issued sideways from the thigh of his predecessor
Than off he starts without a qualm
To hold the one and only lighted candle of the sun in his socket-tip.
He casually gives birth to another young bud from his thigh,
Which at once sets off to be the one and only,
And hold the lighted candle of the sun.

Oh many-branching candelabrum, oh strange up-starting fig-tree,
Oh weird Demos, where every twig is the arch twig,
Each imperiously over-equal to each, equality over-reaching itself
Like the snakes on Medusa's head,
Oh naked fig-tree!

Still, no doubt every one of you can be the sun-socket as well as every
      other of you.
Demos, Demos, Demos!
Demon, too,
Wicked fig-tree, equality puzzle, with your self-conscious secret fruits.

Taormina

Bare Almond-Trees

Wet almond-trees, in the rain,
Like iron sticking grimly out of earth;
Black almond trunks, in the rain,
Like iron implements twisted, hideous, out of the earth,
Out of the deep, soft fledge of Sicilian winter-green,
Earth-grass uneatable,
Almond trunks curving blackly, iron-dark, climbing the slopes.

Almond-tree, beneath the terrace rail,
Black, rusted, iron trunk,
You have welded your thin stems finer,
Like steel, like sensitive steel in the air,
Grey, lavender, sensitive steel, curving thinly and brittly up in a
       parabola.

What are you doing in the December rain.
Have you a strange electric sensitiveness in your steel tips?
Do you feel the air for electric influences
Like some strange magnetic apparatus?
Do you take in messages, in some strange code,
From heaven's wolfish, wandering electricity, that prowls so
       constantly round Etna?
Do you take the whisper of sulphur from the air?
Do you hear the chemical accents of the sun?
Do you telephone the roar of the waters over the earth?
And from all this, do you make calculations?

Sicily, December's Sicily in a mass of rain
With iron branching blackly, rusted like old, twisted implements
And brandishing and stooping over earth's wintry Hedge, climbing
       the slopes
Of uneatable soft green!

Taormina

Tropic

Sun, dark sun
Sun of black void heat
Sun of the torrid mid-day's horrific darkness.

Behold my hair twisting and going black.
Behold my eyes turn tawny yellow
Negroid;
See the milk of northern spume
Coagulating and going black in my veins
Aromatic as frankincense.

Columns dark and soft
Sunblack men
Soft shafts, sunbreathing mouths
Eyes of yellow, golden sand
As frictional, as perilous, explosive as brimstone.

Rock, waves of dark heat;
Waves of dark heat, rock, sway upwards
Waver perpendicular.

What is the horizontal rolling of water
Compared to the flood of black heat that rolls upward past my eyes?

Taormina

Southern Night

Come up, thou red thing.
Come up, and be called a moon.

The mosquitoes are biting to-night
Like memories.

Memories, northern memories,
Bitter-stinging white world that bore us
Subsiding into this night.

Call it moonrise
This red anathema?

Rise, thou red thing,
Unfold slowly upwards, blood-dark;
Burst the night's membrane of tranquil stars
Finally.

Maculate
The red Macula.

Taormina

FLOWERS

"And long ago, the almond was the symbol of resurrection. But tell me, tell me, why should the almond be the symbol of resurrection?

Have you not seen, in the wild winter sun of the southern Mediterranean, in January and in February, the re-birth of the almond tree, all standing in clouds of glory?

Ah yes! ah yes! would I might see it again!

Yet even this is not the secret of the secret. Do you know what was called the almond bone, in the body, the last bone of the spine? This was the seed of the body, and from the grave it could grow into a body again, like almond blossom in January.

No, no, I know nothing of that."

"Oh Persephone, Persephone, bring back to me from Hades the life of a dead man."

"Wretches, utter wretches, keep your hands from beans!" saith Empedokles.

For according to some, the beans were the beans of votes, and votes were politics. But others say it was a food-taboo. Others also say the bean was one of the oldest symbols of the male organ, for the peas-cod is later than the beans-cod."

"But blood is red, and blood is life. Red was the colour of kings. Kings, far-off kings, painted their faces vermilion, and were almost gods."

Almond Blossom

Even iron can put forth,
Even iron.

This is the iron age,
But let us take heart
Seeing iron break and bud,
Seeing rusty iron puff with clouds of blossom.

The almond-tree,
December's bare iron hooks sticking out of earth.

The almond-tree,
That knows the deadliest poison, like a snake
In supreme bitterness.

Upon the iron, and upon the steel,
Odd flakes as if of snow, odd bits of snow.
Odd crumbs of melting snow.

But you mistake, it is not from the sky;
From out the iron, and from out the steel.
Flying not down from heaven, but storming up,
Strange storming up from the dense under-earth
Along the iron, to the living steel
In rose-hot tips, and flakes of rose-pale snow
Setting supreme annunciation to the world.

Nay, what a heart of delicate super-faith,
Iron-breaking,
The rusty swords of almond-trees.

Trees suffer, like races, down the long ages.
They wander and are exiled, they live in exile through long ages
Like drawn blades never sheathed, hacked and gone black,
The alien trees in alien lands: and yet
The heart of blossom,
The unquenchable heart of blossom!

Look at the many-cicatrised frail vine, none more scarred and frail,
Yet see him fling himself abroad in fresh abandon
From the small wound-stump.

Even the wilful, obstinate, gummy fig-tree
Can be kept down, but he'll burst like a polyp into prolixity.

And the almond-tree, in exile, in the iron age!

This is the ancient southern earth whence the vases were baked,
        amphoras, craters, cantharus, œnochœ, and open-hearted cylix,
Bristling now with the iron of almond-trees

Iron, but unforgotten,
Iron, dawn-hearted,
Ever-beating dawn-heart, enveloped in iron against the exile, against
        the ages.

See it come forth in blossom
From the snow-remembering heart
In long-nighted January
In the long dark nights of the evening star, and Sirius, and the Etna
        snow-wind through the long night.

Sweating his drops of blood through the long-nighted Gethsemane
Into blossom into pride, into honey-triumph, into most exquisite
        splendour.
Oh, give me the tree of life in blossom
And the Cross sprouting its superb and fearless flowers!

Something must be reassuring to the almond, in the evening star, and
        the snow-wind, and the long, long, nights,
Some memory of far, sun-gentler lands,
So that the faith in his heart smiles again
And his blood ripples with that untellable delight of once more
        vindicated faith,
And the Gethsemane blood at the iron pores unfolds, unfolds,
Pearls itself into tenderness of bud
And in a great and sacred forthcoming steps forth, steps out in one stride

A naked tree of blossom, like a bridegroom bathing in dew, divested
          of cover,
Frail-naked, utterly uncovered
To the green night-baying of the dog-star, Etna's snow-edged wind
And January's loud-seeming sun.

Think of it, from the iron fastness
Suddenly to dare to come out naked, in perfection of blossom,
          beyond the sword-rust.
Think, to stand there in full-unfolded nudity, smiling,
With all the snow-wind, and the sun-glare, and the dog-star baying
          epithalamion.

Oh, honey-bodied beautiful one,
Come forth from iron,
Red your heart is.
Fragile-tender, fragile-tender life-body,
More fearless than iron all the time,
And so much prouder, so disdainful of reluctances.

In the distance like hoar-frost, like silvery ghosts communing on a
          green hill,
Hoar-frost-like and mysterious.

In the garden raying out
With a body like spray, dawn-tender, and looking about
With such insuperable, subtly-smiling assurance,
Sword-blade-born.

Unpromised,
No bounds being set.
Flaked out and come unpromised,
The tree being life-divine,
Fearing nothing, life-blissful at the core
Within iron and earth.

Knots of pink, fish-silvery
In heaven, in blue, blue heaven,
Soundless, bliss-full, wide-rayed, honey-bodied,

Red at the core,
Red at the core,
Knotted in heaven upon the fine light.

Open,
Open,
Five times wide open,
Six times wide open,
And given, and perfect;
And red at the core with the last sore-heartedness,
Sore-hearted-looking.

Fontana Vecchia

Purple Anemones

Who gave us flowers?
Heaven? The white God?

Nonsense I
Up out of hell,
From Hades;
Infernal Dis!

Jesus the god of flowers——?
Not he.
Or sun-bright Apollo, him so musical?
Him neither.

Who then?
Say who.
Say it—and it is Pluto,
Dis,
The dark one,
Proserpine's master.

Who contradicts——?

When she broke forth from below,
Flowers came, hell-hounds on her heels.
Dis, the dark, the jealous god, the husband,
Flower-sumptuous-blooded.

Go then, he said.
And in Sicily, on the meadows of Enna,
She thought she had left him;
But opened around her purple anemones,
Caverns,
Little hells of colour, caves of darkness,
Hell, risen in pursuit of her; royal, sumptuous
Pit-falls.

All at her feet
Hell opening;
At her white ankles
Hell rearing its husband-splendid, serpent heads,
Hell-purple, to get at her—
Why did he let her go?
So he could track her down again, white victim.

Ah mastery!
Hell's husband-blossoms
Out on earth again.

Look out, Persephone!
You, Madame Ceres, mind yourself, the enemy is upon you.
About your feet spontaneous aconite,
Hell-glamorous, and purple husband-tyranny
Enveloping your late-enfranchised plains.

You thought your daughter had escaped?
No more stockings to darn for the (lower-roots, down in hell?
But ah my dear!

Aha, the stripe-cheeked whelps, whippet-slim crocuses,
At 'em, boys, at 'em!
Ho, golden-spaniel, sweet alert narcissus,
Smell 'em, smell 'em out!

Those two enfranchised women.

Somebody is coming!
Oho there!

Dark blue anemones!
Hell is up!
Hell on earth, and Dis within the depths!

Run, Persephone, he is after you already.

54

Why did he let her go?
To track her down;
All the sport of summer and spring, and flowers snapping at her
        ankles and catching her by the hair!
Poor Persephone and her rights for women.

Husband-snared hell-queen,
It is spring.

It is spring,
And pomp of husband-strategy on earth.

Ceres, kiss your girl, you think you've got her back.
The bit of husband-tilth she is,
Persephone!

Poor mothers-in-law!
They are always sold.

It is spring.

Taormina

Sicilian Cyclamens

When he pushed his bush of black hair off his brow:
When she lifted her mop from her eyes, and screwed it in a knob behind
         —O act of fearful temerity!
When they felt their foreheads bare, naked to heaven, their eyes revealed:
When they felt the light of heaven brandished like a knife at their
      defenceless eyes,
And the sea like a blade at their face,
Mediterranean savages:
When they came out, face-revealed, under heaven, from the shaggy
      undergrowth of their own hair
For the first time,
They saw tiny rose cyclamens between their toes, growing
Where the slow toads sat brooding on the past.

Slow toads, and cyclamen leaves
Stickily glistening with eternal shadow
Keeping to earth.
Cyclamen leaves
Toad-filmy, earth-iridescent
Beautiful
Frost-filigreed
Spumed with mud
Snail-nacreous
Low down.

The shaking aspect of the sea
And man's defenceless bare face
And cyclamens putting their ears back.

Long, pensive, slim-muzzled greyhound buds
Dreamy, not yet present,
Drawn out of earth
At his toes.

Dawn-rose
Sub-delighted, stone-engendered
Cyclamens, young cyclamens

Arching
Waking, pricking their ears
Like delicate very-young greyhound bitches
Half-yawning at the open, inexperienced
Vista of day,
Folding back their soundless petalled ears.

Greyhound bitches
Bending their rosy muzzled pensive down.
And breathing soft, unwilling to wake to the new day
Yet sub-delighted.

Ah Mediterranean morning, when our world began!
Far-off Mediterranean mornings,
Pelasgic faces uncovered,
And unbudding cyclamens.

The hare suddenly goes uphill
Laying back tier long ears with unwinking bliss.

And up the pallid, sea-blenched Mediterranean stone-slopes
Rose cyclamen, ecstatic fore-runner!
Cyclamens, ruddy-muzzled cyclamens
In little bunches like bunches of wild hares
Muzzles together, ears-aprick
Whispering witchcraft
Like women at a well, the dawn-fountain.

Greece, and the world's morning
Where all the Parthenon marbles still fostered the roots of the
        cyclamen.
Violets
Pagan, rosy-muzzled violets
Autumnal
Dawn-pink,
Dawn-pale
Among squat toad-leaves sprinkling the unborn
Erechtheion marbles.

Taormina

Hibiscus and Salvia Flowers

Hark! Hark!
The dogs do bark!
It's the socialists come to town,
None in rags and none in tags,
Swaggering up and down.

Sunday morning,
And from the Sicilian townlets skirting Etna
The socialists have gathered upon us, to look at us.

How shall we know them when we see them?
How shall we know them now they've come?

Not by their rags and not by their tags,
Nor by any distinctive gown;
The same unremarkable Sunday suit
And hats cocked up and down.

Yet there they are, youths, loutishly
Strolling in gangs and staring along the Corso
With the gang-stare
And a half-threatening envy
At every *forestiere*,
Every lordly tuppenny foreigner from the hotels, fattening on the
        exchange.

Hark! Hark!
The dogs do bark!
It's the socialists in the town.
Sans rags, sans tags,
Sans beards, sans bags,
Sans any distinction at all except loutish commonness.

How do we know then, that they are they?
Bolshevists.
Leninists.
Communists.

Socialists.
-Ists! -Ists!

Alas, salvia and hibiscus flowers.
Salvia and hibiscus flowers.

Listen again.
Salvia and hibiscus flowers.
Is it not so?
Salvia and hibiscus flowers.

Hark! Hark!
The dogs do bark!
Salvia and hibiscus flowers.

Who smeared their doors with blood?
Who on their breasts
Put salvias and hibiscus?

Rosy, rosy scarlet,
And flame-rage, golden-throated
Bloom along the Corso on the living, perambulating bush.

Who said they might assume these blossoms?
What god did they consult?

Rose-red, princess hibiscus, rolling her pointed Chinese petals!
Azalea and camellia, single peony
And pomegranate bloom and scarlet mallow-flower
And all the eastern, exquisite royal plants
That noble blood has brought us down the ages!
Gently nurtured, frail and splendid
Hibiscus flower—
Alas, the Sunday coats of Sicilian bolshevists!

Pure blood, and noble blood, in the fine and rose-red veins;
Small, interspersed with jewels of white gold
Frail-filigreed among the rest;
Rose of the oldest races of princesses, Polynesian
Hibiscus.

Eve, in her happy moments.
Put hibiscus in her hair,
Before she humbled herself, and knocked her knees with repentance.

Sicilian bolshevists,
With hibiscus flowers in the buttonholes of your Sunday suits,
Come now, speaking of rights, what right have you to this flower?

The exquisite and ageless aristocracy
Of a peerless soul,
Blessed are the pure in heart and the fathomless in bright pride;
The loveliness that knows *noblesse oblige*;
The native royalty of red hibiscus flowers;
The exquisite assertion of new delicate life
Risen from the roots:
Is this how you'll have it, red-decked socialists,
Hibiscus-breasted?

If it be so, I fly to join you,
And if it be not so, brutes to pull down hibiscus flowers!

Or salvia!
Or dragon-mouthed salvia with gold throat of wrath!
Flame-flushed, enraged, splendid salvia,
Cock-crested, crowing your orange scarlet like a tocsin
Along the Corso all this Sunday morning.

Is your wrath red as salvias,
You socialists?
You with your grudging, envious, furtive rage,
In Sunday suits and yellow boots along the Corso.
You look well with your salvia flowers, I must say.
Warrior-like, dawn-cock's-comb flaring flower
Shouting forth flame to set the world on fire.
The dust heap of man's filthy world on fire.
And burn it down, the glutted, stuffy world.
And feed the young new fields of life with ash,
With ash I say,
Bolshevists,

Your ashes even, my friends,
Among much other ash.

If there were salvia-savage bolshevists
To burn the world back to manure-good ash,
Wouldn't I stick the salvia in my coat!
But these themselves must burn, these louts!

The dragon-faced,
The anger-reddened, golden-throated salvia
With its long antennae of rage put out
Upon the frightened air.
Ugh, how I love its fangs of perfect rage
That gnash the air;
The molten gold of its intolerable rage
Hot in the throat.

I long to be a bolshevist
And set the stinking rubbish-heap of this foul world
Afire at a myriad scarlet points,
A bolshevist, a salvia-face
To lick the world with flame that licks it clean.

I long to see its chock-full crowdedness
And glutted squirming populousness on fire
Like a field of filthy weeds
Burnt back to ash,
And then to see the new, real souls sprout up.

Not this vast rotting cabbage patch we call the world;
But from the ash-scarred fallow
New wild souls.

Nettles, and a rose sprout,
Hibiscus, and mere grass,
Salvia still in a rage
And almond honey-still,
And fig-wort stinking for the carrion wasp;
All the lot of them, and let them fight it out.

But not a trace of foul equality,
Nor sound of still more foul human perfection.
You need not clear the world like a cabbage patch for me;
Leave me my nettles,
Let me fight the wicked, obstreperous weeds myself, and put them in
       their place,
Severely in their place.
I don't at all want to annihilate them,
I like a row with them.
But I won't be put on a cabbage-idealistic level of equality with them.

What rot, to see the cabbage and hibiscus-tree
As equals!
What rot, to say the louts along the Corso
In Sunday suits and yellow shoes
Are my equals!
I am their superior, saluting the hibiscus flower, not them.
The same I say to the profiteers from the hotels, the money-fat-ones,
Profiteers here being called dog-fish, stinking dog-fish, sharks.
The same I say to the pale and elegant persons,
Pale-face authorities loitering tepidly:
That I salute the red hibiscus flowers
And send mankind to its inferior blazes.
Mankind's inferior blazes,
And these along with it, all the inferior lot—
These bolshevists,
These dog-fish,
These precious and ideal ones,
All rubbish ready for fire.

And I salute hibiscus and the salvia flower
Upon the breasts of loutish bolshevists,
Damned loutish bolshevists,
Who perhaps will do the business after all,
In the long run, in spite of themselves.

Meanwhile, alas
For me no fellow-men,
No salvia-frenzied comrades, antennae

Of yellow-red, outreaching, living wrath
Upon the smouldering air,
And throat of brimstone-molten angry gold.
Red, angry men are a race extinct, alas!

Never
To be a bolshevist
With a hibiscus flower behind my ear
In sign of life, of lovely, dangerous life
And passionate disquality of men;
In sign of dauntless, silent violets,
And impudent nettles grabbing the under-earth,
And cabbages born to be cut and eat,
And salvia fierce to crow and shout for fight,
And rosy-red hibiscus wincingly
Unfolding all her coiled and lovely self
In a doubtful world.

Never, bolshevistically
To be able to stand for all these!
Alas, alas, I have got to leave it all
To the youths in Sunday suits and yellow shoes
Who have pulled down the salvia flowers
And rosy delicate hibiscus flowers
And everything else to their disgusting level,
Never, of course, to put anything up again.

But yet
If they pull all the world down,
The process will amount to the same in the end.
Instead of flame and flame-clean ash
Slow watery rotting back to level muck
And final humus,
Whence the re-start.

And still I cannot bear it
That they take hibiscus and the salvia flower.

Taormina

THE EVANGELISTIC BEASTS

"Oh put them back, put them back in the four corners of the heavens, where they belong, the Apocalyptic beasts. For with their wings full of stars they rule the night, and man that watches through the night lives four lives, and man that sleeps through the night sleeps four sleeps, the sleep of the lion, the sleep of the bull, the sleep of the man, and the eagle's sleep. After which the lion wakes, and it is day. Then from the four quarters the four winds blow, and life has its changes. But when the heavens are empty, empty of the four great Beasts, the four Natures, the four Winds, the four Quarters, then sleep is empty too, man sleeps no more like the lion and the bull, nor wakes from the light-eyed eagle sleep."

St Matthew

They are not all beasts.
One is a man, for example, and one is a bird.

I, Matthew, am a man.

"And I, if I be lifted up, will draw all men unto me"—

That is Jesus.
But then Jesus was not quite a man.
He was the Son of Man
Filius Meus, O remorseless logic
Out of His own mouth.

I, Matthew, being a man
Cannot be lifted up, the Paraclete
To draw all men unto me,
Seeing I am on a par with all men.

I, on the other hand.
Am drawn to the Uplifted, as all men are drawn,
To the Son of Man
Filius Meus.

Wilt thou lift me up, Sun of Man?
How my heart beats!
I am man.

I am man, and therefore my heart beats, and throws the dark blood
        from side to side
All the time I am lifted up.
Yes, even during my uplifting.

And if it ceased?
If it ceased, I should be no longer man
As I am, if my heart in uplifting ceased to beat, to toss the dark blood
        from side to side, causing my myriad secret streams.

After the cessation
I might be a soul in bliss, an angel, approximating to the Uplifted;
But that is another matter;
I am Matthew, the man,
And I am not that other angelic matter.

So I will be lifted up. Saviour,
But put me down again in time. Master,
Before my heart stops beating, and I become what I am not.
Put me down again on the earth, Jesus, on the brown soil
Where flowers sprout in the acrid humus, and fade into humus again.
Where beasts drop their unlicked young, and pasture, and drop their
      droppings among the turf.
Where the adder darts horizontal.
Down on the damp, unceasing ground, where my feet belong
And even my heart. Lord, forever, after all uplifting:
The crumbling, damp, fresh land, life horizontal and ceaseless.

Matthew I am, the man.
And I take the wings of the morning, to Thee, Crucified, Glorified.
But while flowers club their petals at evening
And rabbits make pills among the short grass
And long snakes quickly glide into the dark hole in the wall, hearing
      man approach,
I must be put down. Lord, in the afternoon,
And at evening I must leave off my wings of the spirit
As I leave off my braces
And I must resume my nakedness like a fish, sinking down the dark
      reversion of night
Like a fish seeking the bottom, Jesus,
ΙΧΘΥΣ
Face downwards
Veering slowly
Down between the steep slopes of darkness, fucus-dark, seaweed-
      fringed valleys of the waters under the sea
Over the edge of the soundless cataract
Into the fathomless, bottomless pit
Where my soul falls in the last throes of bottomless convulsion, and
      is fallen

Utterly beyond Thee, Dove of the Spirit;
Beyond everything, except itself.

Nay, Son of Man, I have been lifted up.
To Thee I rose like a rocket ending in mid-heaven.
But even Thou, Son of Man, canst not quaff out the dregs of
       terrestrial manhood!
They fall back from Thee.

They fall back, and like a dripping of quicksilver taking the downward
       track,
Break into drops, burn into drops of blood, and dropping, dropping
       take wing
Membraned, blood-veined wings.
On fans of unsuspected tissue, like bats
They thread and thrill and flicker ever downward
To the dark zenith of Thine antipodes
Jesus Uplifted.

Bat-winged heart of man
Reversed flame
Shuddering a strange way down the bottomless pit
To the great depths of its reversed zenith.

Afterwards, afterwards
Morning comes, and I shake the dews of night from the wings of my
       spirit
And mount like a lark, Beloved.

But remember, Saviour,
That my heart which like a lark at heaven's gate singing, hovers
       morning-bright to Thee,
Throws still the dark blood back and forth
In the avenues where the bat hangs sleeping, upside-down
And to me undeniable, Jesus.

Listen, Paraclete.
I can no more deny the bat-wings of my fathom-flickering spirit of
       darkness
Than the wings of the Morning and Thee, Thou Glorified.

I am Matthew, the Man:
It is understood.
And Thou art Jesus, Son of Man
Drawing all men unto Thee, but bound to release them when the
        hour strikes.

I have been, and I have returned.
I have mounted up on the wings of the morning, and I have dredged
        down to the zenith's reversal.
Which is my way, being man.
Gods may stay in mid-heaven, the Son of Man has climbed to the
Whitsun zenith,
But I, Matthew, being a man
Am a traveller back and forth.
So be it.

St Mark

There was a lion in Judah
Which whelped, and was Mark.

But winged.
A lion with wings.
At least at Venice.
Even as late as Daniele Manin.

Why should he have wings?
Is he to be a bird also?
Or a spirit?
Or a winged thought?
Or a soaring consciousness?

Evidently he is all that
The lion of the spirit.

Ah, Lamb of God
Would a wingless lion lie down before Thee, as this winged lion lies?

The lion of the spirit.

Once he lay in the mouth of a cave
And sunned his whiskers,
And lashed his tail slowly, slowly
Thinking of voluptuousness
Even of blood.

But later, in the sun of the afternoon
Having tasted all there was to taste, and having slept his fill
He fell to frowning, as he lay with his head on his paws
And the sun coming in through the narrowest fibril of a slit in his eyes.

So, nine-tenths asleep, motionless, bored, and statically angry,
He saw in a shaft of light a lamb on a pinnacle, balancing a flag on its
      paw,
And he was thoroughly startled.

Going out to investigate
He found the lamb beyond him, on the inaccessible pinnacle of light.
So he put his paw to his nose, and pondered.

"Guard my sheep," came the silvery voice from the pinnacle,
"And I will give thee the wings of the morning."
So the lion of the senses thought it was worth it.

Hence he became a curly sheep-dog with dangerous propensities
As Carpaccio will tell you:
Ramping round, guarding the flock of mankind,
Sharpening his teeth on the wolves,
Ramping up through the air like a kestrel
And lashing his tail above the world
And enjoying the sensation of heaven and righteousness and
        voluptuous wrath.
There is a new sweetness in his voluptuously licking his paw
Now that it is a weapon of heaven.
There is a new ecstasy in his roar of desirous love
Now that it sounds self-conscious through the unlimited sky.
He is well aware of himself
And he cherishes voluptuous delights, and thinks about them
And ceases to be a blood-thirsty king of beasts
And becomes the faithful sheep-dog of the Shepherd, thinking of his
        voluptuous pleasures of chasing the sheep to the fold
And increasing the flock, and perhaps giving a real nip here and there,
        a real pinch, but always well meant.

And somewhere there is a lioness
The she-mate.
Whelps play between the paws of the lion
The she-mate purrs
Their castle is impregnable, their cave,
The sun comes in their lair, they are well-off
A well to do family.

Then the proud lion stalks abroad, alone
And roars to announce himself to the wolves
And also to encourage the red-cross Lamb
And also to ensure a goodly increase in the world.

Look at him, with his paw on the world
At Venice and elsewhere.
Going blind at last.

St Luke

A wall, a bastion,
A living forehead with its slow whorl of hair
And a bull's large, sombre, glancing eye
And glistening, adhesive muzzle
With cavernous nostrils where the winds run hot
Snorting defiance
Or greedily snuffling behind the cows.

Horns
The golden horns of power,
Power to kill, power to create
Such as Moses had, and God,
Head-power.

Shall great wings flame from his shoulder-sockets
Assyrian-wise?
It would be no wonder.

Knowing the thunder of his heart
The massive thunder of his dew-lapped chest
Deep and reverberating,
It would be no wonder if great wings, like flame, fanned out from the
          furnace-cracks of his shoulder-sockets.

Thud! Thud! Thud!
And the roar of black bull's blood in the mighty passages of his chest.
Ah, the dewlap swings pendulous with excess.
The great, roaring weight above
Like a furnace dripping a molten drip.

The urge, the massive, burning ache
Of the bull's breast.
The open furnace-doors of his nostrils.

For what does he ache, and groan?

Is his breast a wall?

Nay, once it was also a fortress wall, and the weight of a vast battery.
But now it is a burning hearthstone only,
Massive old altar of his own burnt offering.

It was always an altar of burnt offering
His own black blood poured out like a sheet of flame over his
          fecundating herd
As he gave himself forth.

But also it was a fiery fortress frowning shaggily on the world
And announcing battle ready.

Since the Lamb bewitched him with that red-struck flag
His fortress is dismantled
His fires of wrath are banked down
His horns turn away from the enemy.

He serves the Son of Man.

And hear him bellow, after many years, the bull that serves the Son
          of Man.
Moaning, booing, roaring hollow
Constrained to pour forth all his fire down the narrow sluice of
          procreation
Through such narrow loins, too narrow.

Is he not over-charged by the dammed-up pressure of his own massive
          black blood
Luke, the Bull, the father of substance, the Providence Bull, after two
          thousand years?
Is he not over-full of offering, a vast, vast offer of himself
Which must be poured through so small a vent?

Too small a vent.

Let him remember his horns, then.
Seal up his forehead once more to a bastion,
Let it know nothing.
Let him charge like a mighty catapult on the red-cross flag, let him
          roar out challenge on the world

And throwing himself upon it, throw off the madness of his blood.
Let it be war.

And so it is war.
The bull of the proletariat has got his head down.

St John

John, oh John,
Thou honourable bird
Sun-peering eagle.

Taking a bird's-eye view
Even of Calvary and Resurrection
Not to speak of Babylon's whoredom.

High over the mild effulgence of the dove
Hung all the time, did we but know it, the all-knowing shadow
Of John's great gold-barred eagle.

John knew all about it
Even the very beginning.

"In the beginning was the Word
And the Word was God
And the Word was with God."

Having been to school
John knew the whole proposition.
As for innocent Jesus
He was one of Nature's phenomena, no doubt.

Oh that mind-soaring eagle of an Evangelist
Staring creation out of countenance
And telling it off
As an eagle staring down on the Sun!

The Logos, the Logos!
"In the beginning was the Word,"

Is there not a great Mind pre-ordaining?
Does not a supreme Intellect ideally procreate the Universe?
Is not each soul a vivid thought in the great consciousness stream of
        God?

Put salt on his tail
The sly bird of John.

Proud intellect, high-soaring Mind
Like a king eagle, bird of the most High, sweeping the round of heaven
And casting the cycles of creation
On two wings, like a pair of compasses;
Jesus' pale and lambent dove, cooing in the lower boughs
On sufferance.

In the beginning was the Word, of course.
And the word was the first offspring of the almighty Johannine mind.
Chick of the intellectual eagle.

Yet put salt on the tail of the Johannine bird
Put salt on its tail
John's eagle.

Shoo it down out of the empyrean
Of the all-seeing, all-fore-ordaining ideal.
Make it roost on bird-spattered, rocky Patmos
And let it moult there, among the stones of the bitter sea.

For the almighty eagle of the fore-ordaining Mind
Is looking rather shabby and island-bound these days:
Moulting, and rather naked about the rump, and down in the beak,
Rather dirty, on dung-whitened Patmos.

From which we are led to assume
That the old bird is weary, and almost willing
That a new chick should chip the extensive shell
Of the mundane egg.

The poor old golden eagle of the creative spirit
Moulting and moping and waiting, willing at last
For the fire to burn it up, feathers and all
So that a new conception of the beginning and end
Can rise from the ashes.

Ah Phoenix, Phoenix
John's Eagle!
You are only known to us now as the badge of an insurance Company.

Phoenix, Phoenix
The nest is in flames
Feathers are singeing,
Ash flutters flocculent, like down on a blue, wan fledgeling.

San Gervasio

CREATURES

"But fishes are very fiery, and take to the water to cool themselves."

"To those things that love darkness, the light of day is cruel and a pain. Yet the light of lamps and candles has no fears for them; rather they draw near to taste it, as if saying: Now what is this? So we see that the sun is more than burning, more than the burning of fires or the shining of lamps. Because with his rays he hurts the creatures that live by night, and lamplight and firelight do them no hurt. Therefore the sun lives in his shining, and is not like fires, that die."

The Mosquito

When did you start your tricks
Monsieur?

What do you stand on such high legs for?
Why this length of shredded shank
You exaltation?

Is it so that you shall lift your centre of gravity upwards
And weigh no more than air as you alight upon me,
Stand upon me weightless, you phantom?

I heard a woman call you the Winged Victory
In sluggish Venice.
You turn your head towards your tail, and smile.

How can you put so much devilry
Into that translucent phantom shred
Of a frail corpus?

Queer, with your thin wings and your streaming legs
How you sail like a heron, or a dull clot of air,
A nothingness.

Yet what an aura surrounds you;
Your evil little aura, prowling, and casting a numbness on my mind.

That is your trick, your bit of filthy magic:
Invisibility, and the anæsthetic power
To deaden my attention in your direction.

But I know your game now, streaky sorcerer.

Queer, how you stalk and prowl the air
In circles and evasions, enveloping me,
Ghoul on wings
Winged Victory.

Settle, and stand on long thin shanks
Eyeing me sideways, and cunningly conscious that I am aware,
You speck.

I hate the way you lurch off sideways into air
Having read my thoughts against you.

Come then, let us play at unawares.
And see who wins in this sly game of bluff.
Man or mosquito.

You don't know that I exist, and I don't know that you exist.
Now then!

It is your trump
It is your hateful little trump
You pointed fiend,
Which shakes my sudden blood to hatred of you:
It is your small, high, hateful bugle in my ear.

Why do you do it?
Surely it is bad policy.

They say you can't help it.

If that is so, then I believe a little in Providence protecting the innocent.
But it sounds so amazingly like a slogan
A yell of triumph as you snatch my scalp.

Blood, red blood
Super-magical
Forbidden liquor.

I behold you stand
For a second enspasmed in oblivion,
Obscenely ecstasied
Sucking live blood
My blood.

Such silence, such suspended transport,
Such gorging,
Such obscenity of trespass.

You stagger
As well as you may.
Only your accursed hairy frailty
Your own imponderable weightlessness
Saves you, wafts you away on the very draught my anger makes in
        its snatching.

Away with a paean of derision
You winged blood-drop.

Can I not overtake you?
Are you one too many for me
Winged Victory?
Am I not mosquito enough to out-mosquito you?

Queer, what a big stain my sucked blood makes
Beside the infinitesimal faint smear of you!
Queer, what a dim dark smudge you have disappeared into!

Siracusa

Fish

Fish, oh Fish,
So little matters!

Whether the waters rise and cover the earth
Or whether the waters wilt in the hollow places,
All one to you.

Aqueous, subaqueous,
Submerged
And wave-thrilled.

As the waters roll
Roll you.
The waters wash,
You wash in oneness
And never emerge.

Never know,
Never grasp.

Your life a sluice of sensation along your sides,
A flush at the flails of your fins, down the whorl of your tail,
And water wetly on fire in the grates of your gills;
Fixed water-eyes.

Even snakes lie together.

But oh, fish, that rock in water.
You lie only with the waters;
One touch.
No fingers, no hands and feet, no lips;
No tender muzzles,
No wistful bellies,
No loins of desire,
None.

You and the naked element,
Sway-wave.
Curvetting bits of tin in the evening light.

Who is it ejects his sperm to the naked flood?
In the wave-mother?
Who swims entombed?
Who lies with the waters of his silent passion, womb-element?
—Fish in the waters under the earth.

What price *his* bread upon the waters?

Himself all silvery himself
In the element
No more.

Nothing more.

Himself,
And the element.
Food, of course!
Water-eager eyes,
Mouth-gate open
And strong spine urging, driving:
And desirous belly gulping.

Fear also!
He knows fear!
Water-eyes craning,
A rush that almost screams,
Almost fish-voice
As the pike comes . . .
Then gay fear, that turns the tail sprightly, from a shadow.

Food, and fear, and joie de vivre,
Without love.

The other way about:
Joie de vivre, and fear, and food,
All without love.

Quelle joie de vivre
Dans l'eau!
Slowly to gape through the waters,
Alone with the element;
To sink, and rise, and go to sleep with the waters;
To speak endless inaudible wavelets into the wave;
To breathe from the flood at the gills,
Fish-blood slowly running next to the flood, extracting fish-fire;
To have the element under one, like a lover;
And to spring away with a curvetting click in the air.
Provocative.
Dropping back with a slap on the face of the flood.
And merging oneself!

To be a fish!

So utterly without misgiving
To be a fish
In the waters.

Loveless, and so lively!
Born before God was love,
Or life knew loving.
Beautifully beforehand with it all.

Admitted, they swarm in companies.
Fishes.
They drive in shoals.
But soundless, and out of contact.
They exchange no word, no spasm, not even anger.
Not one touch.
Many suspended together, forever apart,
Each one alone with the waters, upon one wave with the rest.

A magnetism in the water between them only.

I saw a water-serpent swim across the Anapo,
And I said to my heart, *look, look at him!*
With his head up, steering like a bird!
He's a rare one, but he belongs . . .

But sitting in a boat on the Zeller lake
And watching the fishes in the breathing waters
Lift and swim and go their way—

I said to my heart, *who are these?*
And my heart couldn't own them . . .

A slim young pike with smart fins
And prey-striped suit, a young cub of a pike
Slouching along away below, half out of sight,
Like a lout on an obscure pavement . . .

Aha, there's somebody in the know!

But watching closer
That motionless deadly motion,
That unnatural barrel body, that long ghoul nose . . .
I left off hailing him.

I had made a mistake, I didn't know him,
This grey, monotonous soul in the water,
This intense individual in shadow,
Fish-alive.

I didn't know his God,
I didn't know his God.

Which is perhaps the last admission that life has to wring out of us.

I saw, dimly,
Once a big pike rush,
And small fish fly like splinters.
And I said to my heart, *there are limits*
To you, my heart;
And to the one God.
Fish are beyond me.

Other Gods
Beyond my range . . . gods beyond my God . . .

They are beyond me, are fishes.
I stand at the pale of my being
And look beyond, and see
Fish, in the outerwards,
As one stands on a bank and looks in.

I have waited with a long rod
And suddenly pulled a gold-and-greenish, lucent fish from below,
And had him fly like a halo round my head,
Lunging in the air on the line.

Unhooked his gorping, water-horny mouth,
And seen his horror-tilted eye,
His red-gold, water-precious, mirror-flat bright eye;
And felt him beat in my hand, with his mucous, leaping life-throb.

And my heart accused itself
Thinking: *I am not the measure of creation.*
This is beyond me, this fish.
His God stands outside my God.

And the gold-and-green pure lacquer-mucus comes off in my hand,
And the red-gold mirror-eye stares and dies,
And the water-suave contour dims.

But not before I have had to know
He was born in front of my sunrise,
Before my day.

He outstarts me.
And I, a many-fingered horror of daylight to him,
Have made him die.

Fishes,
With their gold, red eyes, and green pure gleam, and under gold.
And their pre-world loneliness,
And more-than-lovelessness,
And white meat;
They move in other circles.

Outsiders.
Water-wayfarers.
Things of one element.
Aqueous,
Each by itself.

Cats, and the Neapolitans,
Sulphur sun-beasts,
Thirst for fish as for more-than-water;
Water-alive
To quench their over-sulphureous lusts.

But I, I only wonder
And don't know.
I don't know fishes.

In the beginning
Jesus was called The Fish . . .
And in the end.

Zell-am-See

Bat

At evening, sitting on this terrace,
When the sun from the west, beyond Pisa, beyond the mountains of
        Carrara
Departs, and the world is taken by surprise . . .

When the tired flower of Florence is in gloom beneath the glowing
Brown hills surrounding . . .

When under the arches of the Ponte Vecchio
A green light enters against stream, flush from the west,
Against the current of obscure Arno . . .

Look up, and you see things flying
Between the day and the night;
Swallows with spools of dark thread sewing the shadows together.

A circle swoop, and a quick parabola under the bridge arches
Where light pushes through;
A sudden turning upon itself of a thing in the air.
A dip to the water.

And you think:
"The swallows are flying so late!"

Swallows?

Dark air-life looping
Yet missing the pure loop . . .
A twitch, a twitter, an elastic shudder in flight
And serrated wings against the sky,
Like a glove, a black glove thrown up at the light,
And falling back.

Never swallows!
Bats!
The swallows are gone.

At a wavering instant the swallows gave way to bats
By the Ponte Vecchio . . .
Changing guard.

Bats, and an uneasy creeping in one's scalp
As the bats swoop overhead!
Flying madly.

Pipistrello!
Black piper on an infinitesimal pipe.
Little lumps that fly in air and have voices indefinite, wildly vindictive;

Wings like bits of umbrella.

Bats!

Creatures that hang themselves up like an old rag, to sleep;
And disgustingly upside down.
Hanging upside down like rows of disgusting old rags
And grinning in their sleep.
Bats!

Not for me!

Man and Bat

When I went into my room, at mid-morning,
Say ten o'clock . . .
My room, a crash-box over that great stone rattle
The Via de' Bardi . . .

When I went into my room at mid-morning
Why? . . . a bird!

A bird
Flying round the room in insane circles.

In insane circles!
. . . A bat!

A disgusting bat
At mid-morning! . . .

Out! Go out!

Round and round and round
With a twitchy, nervous, intolerable flight,
And a neurasthenic lunge,
And an impure frenzy;
A bat, big as a swallow.

Out, out of my room!

The venetian shutters I push wide
To the free, calm upper air;
Loop back the curtains . . .

Now out, out from my room!

So to drive him out, flicking with my white handkerchief: *Go!*
But he will not.

Round and round and round
In an impure haste,

Fumbling, a beast in air,
And stumbling, lunging and touching the walls, the bell-wires
About my room!

Always refusing to go out into the air
Above that crash-gulf of the Via de' Bardi,
Yet blind with frenzy, with cluttered fear.

At last he swerved into the window bay,
But blew back, as if an incoming wind blew him in again.
A strong inrushing wind.

And round and round and round!
Blundering more insane, and leaping, in throbs, to clutch at a corner,
At a wire, at a bell-rope:
On and on, watched relentless by me, round and round in my room,
Round and round and dithering with tiredness and haste and
            increasing delirium
Flicker-splashing round my room.

I would not let him rest;
Not one instant cleave, cling like a blot with his breast to the wall
In an obscure corner.
Not an instant!

I flicked him on,
Trying to drive him through the window.

Again he swerved into the window bay
And I ran forward, to frighten him forth.
But he rose, and from a terror worse than me he flew past me
Back into my room, and round, round, round in my room
Clutch, cleave, stagger,
Dropping about the air
Getting tired.

Something seemed to blow him back from the window
Every time he swerved at it;
Back on a strange parabola, then round, round, dizzy in my room.

He *could* not go out,
I also realised ...
It was the light of day which he could not enter,
Any more than I could enter the white-hot door of a blast-furnace.

He could not plunge into the daylight that streamed at the window.
It was asking too much of his nature.

Worse even than the hideous terror of me with my handkerchief
Saying: *Out, go out!* ...
Was the horror of white daylight in the window!

So I switched on the electric light, thinking: *Now*
The outside will seem brown ...

But no.
The outside did not seem brown.
And he did not mind the yellow electric light.

Silent!
He was having a silent rest.
But *never!*
Not in *my* room.

Round and round and round
Near the ceiling as if in a web,
Staggering;
Plunging, falling out of the web,
Broken in heaviness,
Lunging blindly,
Heavier;
And clutching, clutching for one second's pause,
Always, as if for one drop of rest,
One little drop.

And I!
Never, I say. . . .
Go out!

Flying slower,
Seeming to stumble, to fall in air.
Blind-weary.

Yet never able to pass the whiteness of light into freedom . . .
A bird would have dashed through, come what might.

Fall, sink, lurch, and round and round
Flicker, flicker-heavy;
Even wings heavy:
And cleave in a high corner for a second, like a clot, also a prayer.

But no.
Out, you beast.

Till he fell in a corner, palpitating, spent.
And there, a clot, he squatted and looked at me.
With sticking-out, bead-berry eyes, black,
And improper derisive ears,
And shut wings,
And brown, furry body.

Brown, nut-brown, fine fur!
But it might as well have been hair on a spider; thing
With long, black-paper ears.

So, a dilemma!
He squatted there like something unclean.

No, he must not squat, nor hang, obscene, in my room!

Yet nothing on earth will give him courage to pass the sweet fire of day.

What then?
Hit him and kill him and throw him away?

Nay,
I didn't create him.
Let the God that created him be responsible for his death . . .
Only, in the bright day, I will not have this clot in my room.

Let the God who is maker of bats watch with them in their unclean
        corners . . .
I admit a God in every crevice,
But not bats in my room;
Nor the God of bats, while the sun shines.

So out, out you brute! . . .
And he lunged, flight-heavy, away from me, sideways, *a sghembo!*
And round and round and round my room, a clot with wings,
Impure even in weariness.

Wings dark skinny and flapping the air,
Lost their flicker.
Spent.

He fell again with a little thud
Near the curtain on the floor.
And there lay.

Ah death, death
You are no solution!
Bats must be bats.

Only life has a way out.
And the human soul is fated to wide-eyed responsibility
In life.

So I picked him up in a flannel jacket,
Well covered, lest he should bite me.
For I would have had to kill him if he'd bitten me, the impure one . . .
And he hardly stirred in my hand, muffled up.

Hastily, I shook him out of the window.

And away he went!
Fear craven in his tail.
Great haste, and straight, almost bird straight above the Via de' Bardi.
Above that crash-gulf of exploding whips,
Towards the Borgo San Jacopo.

And now, at evening, as he flickers over the river
Dipping with petty triumphant flight, and tittering over the sun's
        departure,
I believe he chirps, pipistrello, seeing me here on this terrace writing:
There he sits, the long loud one!
But I am greater than he . . .
I escaped him . . .

Florence

REPTILES

"Homer was wrong in saying, 'Would that strife might pass away from among gods and men!' He did not see that he was praying for the destruction of the universe; for, if his prayer were heard, all things would pass away—for in the tension of opposites all things have their being—"

"For when Fire in its downward path chanced to mingle with the dark breath of the earth, the serpent slid forth, lay revealed. But he was moist and cold, the sun in him darted uneasy, held down by moist earth, never could he rise on his feet. And this is what put poison in his mouth. For the sun in him would fain rise half-way, and move on feet. But moist earth weighs him down, though he dart and twist, still he must go with his belly on the ground. The wise tortoise laid his earthy part around him, he cast it round him and found his feet. So he is the first of creatures to stand upon his toes, and the dome of his house is his heaven. Therefore it is charted out, and is the foundation of the world."

Snake

A snake came to my water-trough
On a hot, hot day, and I in pyjamas for the heat,
To drink there.

In the deep, strange-scented shade of the great dark carob-tree
I came down the steps with my pitcher
And must wait, must stand and wait, for there he was at the trough
         before me.

He reached down from a fissure in the earth-wall in the gloom
And trailed his yellow-brown slackness soft-bellied down, over the
         edge of the stone trough
And rested his throat upon the stone bottom,
And where the water had dripped from the tap, in a small clearness,
He sipped with his straight mouth,
Softly drank through his straight gums, into his slack long body,
Silently.

Someone was before me at my water-trough.
And I, like a second comer, waiting.

He lifted his head from his drinking, as cattle do.
And looked at me vaguely, as drinking cattle do,
And flickered his two-forked tongue from his lips, and mused a
         moment,
And stooped and drank a little more,
Being earth-brown, earth-golden from the burning bowels of the earth
On the day of Sicilian July, with Etna smoking.

The voice of my education said to me
He must be killed,
For in Sicily the black, black snakes are innocent, the gold are
         venomous.

And voices in me said, If you were a man
You would take a stick and break him now, and finish him off.

But must I confess how I liked him,
How glad I was he had come like a guest in quiet, to drink at my
            water-trough
And depart peaceful, pacified, and thankless,
Into the burning bowels of this earth?

Was it cowardice, that I dared not kill him?
Was it perversity, that I longed to talk to him?
Was it humility, to feel so honoured?
I felt so honoured.

And yet those voices:
If you were not afraid, you would kill him!

And truly I was afraid, I was most afraid,
But even so, honoured still more
That he should seek my hospitality
From out the dark door of the secret earth.

He drank enough
And lifted his head, dreamily, as one who has drunken,
And flickered his tongue like a forked night on the air, so black,
Seeming to lick his lips.
And looked around like a god, unseeing, into the air,
And slowly turned his head,
And slowly, very slowly, as if thrice adream,
Proceeded to draw his slow length curving round
And climb again the broken bank of my wall-face.

And as he put his head into that dreadful hole,
And as he slowly drew up, snake-easing his shoulders, and entered
            farther,
A sort of horror, a sort of protest against his withdrawing into that
            horrid black hole,
Deliberately going into the blackness, and slowly drawing himself after,
Overcame me now his back was turned.

I looked round, I put down my pitcher,
I picked up a clumsy log
And threw it at the water-trough with a clatter.

I think it did not hit him,
But suddenly that part of him that was left behind convulsed in
        undignified haste,
Writhed like lightning, and was gone
Into the black hole, the earth-lipped fissure in the wall-front,
At which, in the intense still noon, I stared with fascination.

And immediately I regretted it.
I thought how paltry, how vulgar, what a mean act!
I despised myself and the voices of my accursed human education.

And I thought of the albatross,
And I wished he would come back, my snake.

For he seemed to me again like a king,
Like a king in exile, uncrowned in the underworld,
Now due to be crowned again.

And so, I missed my chance with one of the lords
Of life.
And I have something to expiate;
A pettiness.

Taormina

Baby Tortoise

You know what it is to be born alone,
Baby tortoise!

The first day to heave your feet little by little from the shell,
Not yet awake,
And remain lapsed on earth,
Not quite alive.

A tiny, fragile, half-animate bean.

To open your tiny beak-mouth, that looks as if it would never open,
Like some iron door;
To lift the upper hawk-beak from the lower base
And reach your skinny little neck
And take your first bite at some dim bit of herbage,
Alone, small insect,
Tiny bright-eye,
Slow one.

To take your first solitary bite
And move on your slow, solitary hunt.
Your bright, dark little eye,
Your eye of a dark disturbed night,
Under its slow lid, tiny baby tortoise,
So indomitable.

No one ever heard you complain.

You draw your head forward, slowly, from your little wimple
And set forward, slow-dragging, on your four-pinned toes,
Rowing slowly forward.
Whither away, small bird?

Rather like a baby working its limbs.
Except that you make slow, ageless progress
And a baby makes none.

The touch of sun excites you.
And the long ages, and the lingering chill
Make you pause to yawn,
Opening your impervious mouth,
Suddenly beak-shaped, and very wide, like some suddenly gaping
          pincers;
Soft red tongue, and hard thin gums,
Then close the wedge of your little mountain front,
Your face, baby tortoise.

Do you wonder at the world, as slowly you turn your head in its wimple
And look with laconic, black eyes?
Or is sleep coming over you again,
The non-life?

You are so hard to wake.

Are you able to wonder?
Or is it just your indomitable will and pride of the first life
Looking round
And slowly pitching itself against the inertia
Which had seemed invincible?

The vast inanimate,
And the fine brilliance of your so tiny eye,
Challenger.

Nay, tiny shell-bird,
What a huge vast inanimate it is, that you must row against,
What an incalculable inertia.

Challenger,
Little Ulysses, fore-runner,
No bigger than my thumb-nail,
Buon viaggio.

All animate creation on your shoulder,
Set forth, little Titan, under your battle-shield.

The ponderous, preponderate.
Inanimate universe;
And you are slowly moving, pioneer, you alone.

How vivid your travelling seems now, in the troubled sunshine,
Stoic, Ulyssean atom;
Suddenly hasty, reckless, on high toes.

Voiceless little bird.
Resting your head half out of your wimple
In the slow dignity of your eternal pause.
Alone, with no sense of being alone,
And hence six times more solitary;
Fulfilled of the slow passion of pitching through immemorial ages
Your little round house in the midst of chaos.

Over the garden earth,
Small bird,
Over the edge of all things.

Traveller,
With your tail tucked a little on one side
Like a gentleman in a long-skirted coat.

All life carried on your shoulder,
Invincible fore-runner.

Tortoise Shell

The Cross, the Cross
Goes deeper in than we know,
Deeper into life;
Right into the marrow
And through the bone.

Along the back of the baby tortoise
The scales are locked in an arch like a bridge,
Scale-lapping, like a lobster's sections
Or a bee's.

Then crossways down his sides
Tiger-stripes and wasp-bands.

Five, and five again, and five again.
And round the edges twenty-five little ones,
The sections of the baby tortoise shell.

Four, and a keystone;
Four, and a keystone;
Four, and a keystone;
Then twenty-four, and a tiny little keystone.

It needed Pythagoras to see life playing with counters on the living back
Of the baby tortoise;
Life establishing the first eternal mathematical tablet,
Not in stone, like the Judean Lord, or bronze, but in life-clouded,
       life-rosy tortoise shell.

The first little mathematical gentleman
Stepping, wee mite, in his loose trousers
Under all the eternal dome of mathematical law.

Fives, and tens,
Threes and fours and twelves,
All the *volte face* of decimals,
The whirligig of dozens and the pinnacle of seven.

Turn him on his back,
The kicking little beetle,
And there again, on his shell-tender, earth-touching belly,
The long cleavage of division, upright of the eternal cross
And on either side count five,
On each side, two above, on each side, two below
The dark bar horizontal.

The Cross!
It goes right through him, the sprottling insect,
Through his cross-wise cloven psyche,
Through his five-fold complex-nature.

So turn him over on his toes again;
Four pin-point toes, and a problematical thumb-piece,
Four rowing limbs, and one wedge-balancing head,
Four and one makes five, which is the clue to all mathematics.

The Lord wrote it all down on the little slate
Of the baby tortoise.
Outward and visible indication of the plan within,
The complex, manifold involvedness of an individual creature
Plotted out
On this small bird, this rudiment,
This little dome, this pediment
Of all creation,
This slow one.

Tortoise Family Connections

On he goes, the little one,
Bud of the universe,
Pediment of life.

Setting off somewhere, apparently,
Whither away, brisk egg?

His mother deposited him on the soil as if he were no more than
      droppings,
And now he scuffles tinily past her as if she were an old rusty tin.

A mere obstacle,
He veers round the slow great mound of her—
Tortoises always foresee obstacles.

It is no use my saying to him in an emotional voice:
"This is your Mother, she laid you when you were an egg."

He does not even trouble to answer: "Woman, what have I to do with
      thee?"
He wearily looks the other way,
And she even more wearily looks another way still,
Each with the utmost apathy,
Incognisant,
Unaware,
Nothing.

As for papa,
He snaps when I offer him his offspring,
Just as he snaps when I poke a hit of stick at him,
Because he is irascible this morning, an irascible tortoise
Being touched with love, and devoid of fatherliness.

Father and mother,
And three little brothers,
And all rambling aimless, like little perambulating pebbles scattered
      in the garden,
Not knowing each other from bits of earth or old tins.

Except that papa and mama are old acquaintances, of course,
Though family feeling there is none, not even the beginnings.

Fatherless, motherless, brotherless, sisterless
Little tortoise.

Row on then, small pebble,
Over the clods of the autumn, wind-chilled sunshine,
Young gaiety.

Does he look for a companion?

No, no, don't think it.
He doesn't know he is alone;
Isolation is his birthright,
This atom.

To row forward, and reach himself tall on spiny toes,
To travel, to burrow into a little loose earth, afraid of the night,
To crop a little substance,
To move, and to be quite sure that he is moving:
Basta!
To be a tortoise!
Think of it, in a garden of inert clods
A brisk, brindled little tortoise, all to himself—
Croesus!

In a garden of pebbles and insects
To roam, and feel the slow heart beat
Tortoise-wise, the first bell sounding
From the warm blood, in the dark-creation morning.

Moving, and being himself,
Slow, and unquestioned,
And inordinately there, O stoic!
Wandering in the slow triumph of his own existence,
Ringing the soundless bell of his presence in chaos,
And biting the frail grass arrogantly,
Decidedly arrogantly.

Lui et elle

She is large and matronly
And rather dirty,
A little sardonic-looking, as if domesticity had driven her to it.

Though what she does, except lay four eggs at random in the garden
          once a year
And put up with her husband,
I don't know.

She likes to eat.
She hurries up, striding reared on long uncanny legs,
When food is going.
Oh yes, she can make haste when she likes.

She snaps the soft bread from my hand in great mouthfuls,
Opening her rather pretty wedge of an iron, pristine face
Into an enormously wide-beaked mouth
Like sudden curved scissors,
And gulping at more than she can swallow, and working her thick,
          soft tongue,
And having the bread hanging over her chin.

O Mistress, Mistress,
Reptile mistress,
Your eye is very dark, very bright,
And it never softens
Although you watch.

She knows,
She knows well enough to come for food,
Yet she sees me not;
Her bright eye sees, but not me, not anything,
Sightful, sightless, seeing and visionless,
Reptile mistress.

Taking bread in her curved, gaping, toothless mouth,
She has no qualm when she catches my finger in her steel
          overlapping gums,

But she hangs on, and my shout and my shrinking are nothing to her.
She does not even know she is nipping me with her curved beak.
Snake-like she draws at my finger, while I drag it in horror away.

Mistress, reptile mistress.
You are almost too large, I am almost frightened.

He is much smaller,
Dapper beside her,
And ridiculously small.

Her laconic eye has an earthy, materialistic look,
His, poor darling, is almost fiery.

His wimple, his blunt-prowed face,
His low forehead, his skinny neck, his long, scaled, striving legs,
So striving, striving,
Are all more delicate than she,
And he has a cruel scar on his shell.

Poor darling, biting at her feet,
Running beside her like a dog, biting her earthy, splay feet,
Nipping her ankles,
Which she drags apathetic away, though without retreating into her
        shell.

Agelessly silent,
And with a grim, reptile determination,
Cold, voiceless age-after-age behind him, serpents' long obstinacy
Of horizontal persistence.

Little old man
Scuffling beside her, bending down, catching his opportunity,
Parting his steel-trap face, so suddenly, and seizing her scaly ankle,
And hanging grimly on,
Letting go at last as she drags away,
And closing his steel-trap face.

His steel-trap, stoic, ageless, handsome face.
Alas, what a fool he looks in this scuffle.

And how he feels it!
The lonely rambler, the stoic, dignified stalker through chaos,
The immune, the animate,
Enveloped in isolation,
Forerunner.
Now look at him!

Alas, the spear is through the side of his isolation.
His adolescence saw him crucified into sex,
Doomed, in the long crucifixion of desire, to seek his consummation
        beyond himself.
Divided into passionate duality,
He, so finished and immune, now broken into desirous
        fragmentariness,
Doomed to make an intolerable fool of himself
In his effort toward completion again.

Poor little earthy house-inhabiting Osiris,
The mysterious bull tore him at adolescence into pieces,
And he must struggle after reconstruction, ignominiously.

And so behold him following the tail
Of that mud-hovel of his slowly rambling spouse,
Like some unhappy bull at the tail of a cow,
But with more than bovine, grim, earth-dank persistence.

Suddenly seizing the ugly ankle as she stretches out to walk,
Roaming over the sods,
Or, if it happen to show, at her pointed, heavy tail
Beneath the low-dropping back-board of her shell.

Their two shells like domed boats bumping,
Hers huge, his small;
Their splay feet rambling and rowing like paddles,
And stumbling mixed up in one another.
In the race of love—
Two tortoises,
She huge, he small.

She seems earthily apathetic,
And he has a reptile's awful persistence.

I heard a woman pitying her, pitying the Mère Tortue.
While I, I pity Monsieur.
"He pesters her and torments her," said the woman.
How much more is he pestered and tormented, say I.

What can he do?
He is dumb, he is visionless,
Conceptionless.
His black, sad-lidded eye sees but beholds not
As her earthen mound moves on,
But he catches the folds of vulnerable, leathery skin,
Nail-studded, that shake beneath her shell,
And drags at these with his beak,
Drags and drags and bites,
While she pulls herself free, and rows her dull mound along.

Tortoise Gallantry

Making his advances
He does not look at her, nor sniff at her,
No, not even sniff at her, his nose is blank.

Only he senses the vulnerable folds of skin
That work beneath her while she sprawls along
In her ungainly pace,
Her folds of skin that work and row
Beneath the earth-soiled hovel in which she moves.

And so he strains beneath her housey walls
And catches her trouser-legs in his beak
Suddenly, or her skinny limb,
And strange and grimly drags at her
Like a dog,
Only agelessly silent, with a reptile's awful persistency

Grim, gruesome gallantry, to which he is doomed.
Dragged out of an eternity of silent isolation
And doomed to partiality, partial being,
Ache, and want of being,
Want,
Self-exposure, hard humiliation, need to add himself on to her.

Born to walk alone,
Fore-runner,
Now suddenly distracted into this mazy side-track,
This awkward, harrowing pursuit,
This grim necessity from within.

Does she know
As she moves eternally slowly away?
Or is he driven against her with a bang, like a bird flying in the dark
            against a window,
All knowledgeless?

The awful concussion,
And the still more awful need to persist, to follow, follow, continue,

Driven, after aeons of pristine, fore-god-like singleness and oneness,
At the end of some mysterious, red-hot iron,
Driven away from himself into her tracks,
Forced to crash against her.

Stiff, gallant, irascible, crook-legged reptile,
Little gentleman,
Sorry plight,
We ought to look the other way.

Save that, having come with you so far,
We will go on to the end.

Tortoise Shout

I thought he was dumb,
I said he was dumb,
Yet I've heard him cry.

First faint scream,
Out of life's unfathomable dawn,
Far off, so far, like a madness, under the horizon's dawning rim,
Far, far off, far scream.

Tortoise *in extremis.*

Why were we crucified into sex?
Why were we not left rounded off, and finished in ourselves,
As we began,
As he certainly began, so perfectly alone?

A far, was-it-audible scream,
Or did it sound on the plasm direct?

Worse than the cry of the new-born,
A scream,
A yell,
A shout,
A pæan,
A death-agony,
A birth-cry,
A submission,
All tiny, tiny, far away, reptile under the first dawn.

War-cry, triumph, acute delight, death-scream reptilian,
Why was the veil torn?
The silken shriek of the soul's torn membrane?
The male soul's membrane
Torn with a shriek half music, half horror.

Crucifixion.
Male tortoise, cleaving behind the hovel-wall of that dense female,

Mounted and tense, spread-eagle, out-reaching out of the shell
In tortoise-nakedness,
Long neck, and long vulnerable limbs extruded, spread-eagle over her
      house-roof,
And the deep, secret, all-penetrating tail curved beneath her walls,
Reaching and gripping tense, more reaching anguish in uttermost tension
Till suddenly, in the spasm of coition, tupping like a jerking leap, and oh!
Opening its clenched face from his outstretched neck
And giving that fragile yell, that scream,
Super-audible,
From his pink, cleft, old-man's mouth,
Giving up the ghost,
Or screaming in Pentecost, receiving the ghost.

His scream, and his moment's subsidence,
The moment of eternal silence,
Yet unreleased, and after the moment, the sudden, startling jerk of
      coition, and at once
The inexpressible faint yell—
And so on, till the last plasm of my body was melted back
To the primeval rudiments of life, and the secret.

So he tups, and screams
Time after time that frail, torn scream
After each jerk, the longish interval,
The tortoise eternity,
Age-long, reptilian persistence,
Heart-throb, slow heart-throb, persistent for the next spasm.

I remember, when I was a boy,
I heard the scream of a frog, which was caught with his foot in the
      mouth of an up-starting snake;
I remember when I first heard bull-frogs break into sound in the spring;
I remember hearing a wild goose out of the throat of night
Cry loudly, beyond the lake of waters;
I remember the first time, out of a bush in the darkness, a nightingale's
      piercing cries and gurgles startled the depths of my soul;
I remember the scream of a rabbit as I went through a wood at midnight;
I remember the heifer in her heat, blorting and blorting through the
      hours, persistent and irrepressible;

I remember my first terror hearing the howl of weird, amorous cats;
I remember the scream of a terrified, injured horse, the sheet-lightning,
And running away from the sound of a woman in labour, something
        like an owl whooing,
And listening inwardly to the first bleat of a lamb,
The first wail of an infant,
And my mother singing to herself,
And the first tenor singing of the passionate throat of a young collier,
        who has long since drunk himself to death,
The first elements of foreign speech
On wild dark lips.

And more than all these,
And less than all these,
This last,
Strange, faint coition yell
Of the male tortoise at extremity,
Tiny from under the very edge of the farthest far-off horizon of life.

The cross,
The wheel on which our silence first is broken,
Sex, which breaks up our integrity, our single inviolability, our deep
        silence
Tearing a cry from us.

Sex, which breaks us into voice, sets us calling across the deeps, calling,
        calling for the complement,
Singing, and calling, and singing again, being answered, having found.

Torn, to become whole again, after long seeking for what is lost,
The same cry from the tortoise as from Christ, the Osiris-cry of
        abandonment,
That which is whole, torn asunder,
That which is in part, finding its whole again throughout the universe.

BIRDS

"Birds are the life of the skies, and when they fly, they reveal the thoughts of the skies. The eagle flies nearest to the sun, no other bird flies so near.

So he brings down the life of the sun, and the power of the sun, in his wings, and men who see him wheeling are filled with the elation of the sun. But all creatures of the sun must dip their mouths in blood, the sun is forever thirsty, thirsting for the brightest exhalation of blood.

You shall know a bird by his cry, and great birds cry loud, but sing not. The eagle screams when the sun is high, the peacock screams at the dawn, rooks call at evening, when the nightingale sings. And all birds have their voices, each means a different thing."

Turkey-Cock

You ruffled black blossom,
You glossy dark wind.

Your sort of gorgeousness,
Dark and lustrous
And skinny repulsive
And poppy-glossy,
Is the gorgeousness that evokes my most puzzled admiration.

Your aboriginality
Deep, unexplained,
Like a Red Indian darkly unfinished and aloof,
Seems like the black and glossy seeds of countless centuries.

Your wattles are the colour of steel-slag which has been red-hot
And is going cold,
Cooling to a powdery, pale-oxydised sky-blue.

Why do you have wattles, and a naked, wattled head?
Why do you arch your naked-set eye with a more-than-comprehensible
        arrogance?

The vulture is bald, so is the condor, obscenely,
But only you have thrown this amazing mantilla of oxydised sky-blue
And hot red over you.

This queer dross shawl of blue and vermilion,
Whereas the peacock has a diadem.

I wonder why.
Perhaps it is a sort of uncanny decoration, a veil of loose skin.
Perhaps it is your assertion, in all this ostentation, of raw
        contradictoriness.
Your wattles drip down like a shawl to your breast
And the point of your mantilla drops across your nose, unpleasantly.

Or perhaps it is something unfinished
A bit of slag still adhering, after your firing in the furnace of creation.

Or perhaps there is something in your wattles of a bull's dew-lap
Which slips down like a pendulum to balance the throbbing mass of
        a generous breast.

The over-drip of a great passion hanging in the balance.
Only yours would be a raw, unsmelted passion, that will not quite fuse
        from the dross.

You contract yourself,
You arch yourself as an archer's bow
Which quivers indrawn as you clench your spine
Until your veiled head almost touches backward
To the root-rising of your erected tail.
And one intense and backward-curving frisson
Seizes you as you clench yourself together
Like some fierce magnet bringing its poles together.

Burning, pale positive pole of your wattled head!
And from the darkness of that opposite one
The upstart of your round-barred, sun-round tail!

Whilst between the two, along the tense arch of your back
Blows the magnetic current in fierce blasts,
Ruffling black, shining feathers like lifted mail,
Shuddering storm wind, or a water rushing through.

Your brittle, super-sensual arrogance
Tosses the crape of red across your brow and down your breast
As you draw yourself upon yourself in insistence.

It is a declaration of such tension in will
As time has not dared to avouch, nor eternity been able to unbend
Do what it may.
A raw American will, that has never been tempered by life;
You brittle, will-tense bird with a foolish eye.

126

The peacock lifts his rods of bronze
And struts blue-brilliant out of the far East.
But watch a turkey prancing low on earth
Drumming his vaulted wings, as savages drum
Their rhythms on long-drawn, hollow, sinister drums.
The ponderous, sombre sound of the great drum of Huichilobos
In pyramid Mexico, during sacrifice.

Drum, and the turkey onrush
Sudden, demonic dauntlessness, full abreast,
All the bronze gloss of all his myriad petals
Each one apart and instant.
Delicate frail crescent of the gentle outline of white
At each feather-tip
So delicate;
Yet the bronze wind-well suddenly clashing
And the eye over-weening into madness.

Turkey-cock, turkey-cock
Are you the bird of the next dawn?

Has the peacock had his day, does he call in vain, screecher, for the
        sun to rise?
The eagle, the dove, and the barnyard rooster, do they call in vain,
        trying to wake the morrow?
And do you await us, wattled father. Westward?
Will your yell do it?

Take up the trail of the vanished American
Where it disappeared at the foot of the crucifix.
Take up the primordial Indian obstinacy,
The more than human, dense insistence of will,
And disdain, and blankness, and onrush, and prise open the new day
        with them?

The East a dead letter, and Europe moribund . . . Is that so?
And those sombre, dead, feather-lustrous Aztecs, Amerindians,
In all the sinister splendour of their red blood sacrifices,
Do they stand under the dawn, half-godly, half-demon, awaiting the
        cry of the turkey-cock?

Or must you go through the fire once more, till you're smelted pure,
Slag-wattled turkey-cock,
Dross-jabot?

Fiesole

Humming-Bird

I can imagine, in some otherworld
Primeval-dumb, far back
In that most awful stillness, that only gasped and hummed,
Humming-birds raced down the avenues.

Before anything had a soul,
While life was a heave of Matter, half inanimate,
This little bit chipped off in brilliance
And went whizzing through the slow, vast, succulent stems.

I believe there were no flowers, then
In the world where the humming-bird flashed ahead of creation.
I believe he pierced the slow vegetable veins with his long beak.

Probably he was big
As mosses, and little lizards, they say were once big.
Probably he was a jabbing, terrifying monster.

We look at him through the wrong end of the long telescope of Time,
Luckily for us.

Española

129

Eagle in New Mexico

Towards the sun, towards the south-west
A scorched breast.
A scorched breast, breasting the sun like an answer,
Like a retort.

An eagle at the top of a low cedar-bush
On the sage-ash desert
Reflecting; the scorch of the sun from his breast;
Eagle, with the sickle dripping darkly above.

Erect, scorched-pallid out of the hair of the cedar,
Erect, with the god-thrust entering him from below,
Eagle gloved in feathers
In scorched white feathers
In burnt dark feathers
In feathers still fire-rusted;
Sickle-overswept, sickle dripping over and above.

Sun-breaster,
Staring two ways at once, Lo right and left;
Masked-one
Dark-visaged
Sickle-masked
With iron between your two eyes;
You feather-gloved
To the feet;
Foot-fierce;
Erect one;
The god-thrust entering you steadily from below.

You never look at the sun with your two eyes.
Only the inner eye of your scorched broad breast
Looks straight at the sun.

You are dark
Except scorch-pale-breasted;
And dark cleaves down and weapon-hard downward curving

At your scorched breast,
Like a sword of Damocles,
Beaked eagle.

You've dipped it in blood so many times
That dark face-weapon, to temper it well,
Blood-thirsty bird.

Why do you front the sun so obstinately,
American eagle?
As if you owed him an old, old grudge, great sun: or an old, old
        allegiance.

When you pick the red smoky heart from a rabbit or a light-blooded
        bird
Do you lift it to the sun, as the Aztec priests used to lift red hearts of
        men?

Does the sun need steam of blood do you think
In America, still,
Old eagle?

Does the sun in New Mexico sail like a fiery bird of prey in the sky
Hovering?

Does he shriek for blood?
Does he fan great wings above the prairie, like a hovering, blood-
        thirsty bird?

And are you his priest, big eagle
Whom the Indians aspire to?
Is there a bond of bloodshed between you?

Is your continent cold from the ice-age still, that the sun is so angry?
Is the blood of your continent somewhat reptilian still,
That the sun should be greedy for it?

I don't yield to you, big, jowl-faced eagle.
Nor you nor your blood-thirsty sun

That sucks up blood
Leaving a nervous people.

Fly off, big bird with a big black back,
Fly slowly away, with a rust of fire in your tail,
Dark as you are on your dark side, eagle of heaven.

Even the sun in heaven can be curbed and chastened at last
By the life in the hearts of men.
And you, great bird, sun-starer, heavy black beak
Can be put out of office as sacrifice bringer.

Taos

The Blue Jay

The blue jay with a crest on his head
Comes round the cabin in the snow.
He runs in the snow like a bit of blue metal,
Turning his back on everything.

From the pine-tree that towers and hisses like a pillar of shaggy cloud
Immense above the cabin
Comes a strident laugh as we approach, this little black dog and I.
So halts the little black bitch on four spread paws in the snow
And looks up inquiringly into the pillar of cloud.
With a tinge of misgiving.
Ca-a-a! comes the scrape of ridicule out of the tree.

What voice of the Lord is that, from the tree of smoke?

Oh Bibbles, little black bitch in the snow,
With a pinch of snow in the groove of your silly snub nose.
What do you look at me for?
What do you look at me for, with such misgiving?

It's the blue jay laughing at us.
It's the blue jay jeering at us, Bibs.

Every day since the snow is here
The blue jay paces round the cabin, very busy, picking up bits,
Turning his back on us all,
And bobbing; his thick dark crest about the snow, as if darkly saying:
I ignore those folk who look out.

You acid-blue metallic bird,
You thick bird with a strong crest
Who are you?
Whose boss are you, with all your bully way?
You copper-sulphate blue-bird!

Lobo

133

Animals

"Yes, and if oxen or lions had hands, and could paint with their hands, and produce works of art as men do, horses would paint the forms of the gods like horses, and oxen like oxen, and make their bodies in the image of their several kinds."

"Once, they say, he was passing by when a dog was being beaten, and he spoke this word: 'Stop! don't beat it! For it is the soul of a friend I recognised when I heard its voice.'"

"Swine wash in mire, and barnyard fowls in dust."

The Ass

The long-drawn bray of the ass
In the Sicilian twilight—

All mares are dead!
All mares are dead!
Oh-h!
Oh-h-h!
Oh-h-h-h-h—h!!
I can't bear it, I can't bear it,
I can't!
Oh, I can't!
Oh—
There's one left!
There's one left!
One!
There's one . . . left . . .

So ending on a grunt of agonised relief.

This is the authentic Arabic interpretation of the braying of the ass.
And Arabs should know.

And yet, as his brass-resonant howling yell resounds through the
          Sicilian twilight
I am not sure—

His big, furry head.
His big, regretful eyes,
His diminished, drooping hindquarters,
His small toes.

Such a dear!
Such an ass!
With such a knot inside him!
He regrets something that he remembers.
That's obvious.

The Steppes of Tartary,
And the wind in his teeth for a bit,
And *noli me tangere*.

Ah then, when he tore the wind with his teeth,
And trod wolves underfoot,
And over-rode his mares as if he were savagely leaping an obstacle, to
      set his teeth in the sun . . .

Somehow, alas, he fell in love,
And was sold into slavery.

He fell into the rut of love,
Poor ass, like man, always in a rut,
The pair of them alike in that.

All his soul in his gallant member
And his head gone heavy with the knowledge of desire
And humiliation.

The ass was the first of all animals to fall finally into love,
From obstacle-leaping pride,
Mare obstacle,
Into love, mare-goal, and the knowledge of love.

Hence Jesus rode him in the Triumphant Entry,
Hence his beautiful eyes.
Hence his ponderous head, brooding over desire, and downfall, Jesus,
      and a pack-saddle,
Hence he uncovers his big ass-teeth and howls in that agony that is
      half-insatiable desire and half- unquenchable humiliation.
Hence the black cross on his shoulders.

The Arabs were only half right, though they hinted the whole;
Everlasting lament in everlasting desire.

See him standing with his head down, near the Porta Cappuccini,
Asinello,
Somaro;

With the half-veiled, beautiful eyes, and the pensive face not asleep,
Motionless, like a bit of rock.

Has he seen the Gorgon's head, and turned to stone?
Alas, Love did it.
Now he's a jackass, a pack-ass, a donkey, somaro, burro, with a boss
        piling loads on his back.
Tied by the nose at the Porta Cappuccini.
And tied in a knot, inside, dead-licked between two desires:
To overleap like a male all mares as obstacles
In a leap at the sun;
And to leap in one last heart-bursting leap like a male at the goal of
        a mare,
And there end.
Well, you can't have it both roads.

Hee! Hee! Ehee! Ehow! Ehaw!! Oh! Oh! Oh-h-h!!
The wave of agony bursts in the stone that he was,
Bares his long ass's teeth, flattens his long ass's ears, straightens his
        donkey neck,
And howls his pandemonium on the indignant air.

Yes, it's a quandary.
Jesus rode on him, the first burden on the first beast of burden.
Love on a submissive ass.
So the tale began.

But the ass never forgets.

The horse, being nothing but a nag, will forget.
And men, being mostly geldings and knacker-boned hacks, have
        almost all forgot.
But the ass is a primal creature, and never forgets.

The Steppes of Tartary,
And Jesus on a meek ass-colt: mares: Mary escaping to Egypt:
        Joseph's cudgel.

Hee! Hee! Ehee! Ehow—ow!-ow!-aw!-aw!-aw!
All mares are dead!

139

Or else I am dead!
One of us, or the pair of us,
I don't know—ow!—ow!
Which!
Not quite sure-ure-ure
Quite which!
Which!

Taormina

He-Goat

See his black nose snubbed back, pressed over like a whale's blow-holes,
As if his nostrils were going to curve back to the root of his tail.

As he charges slow among the herd
And rows among the females like a ship pertinaciously,
Heavy with a rancid cargo, through the lesser ships—
Old father
Sniffing forever ahead of him, at the rear of the goats, that they lift
       the little door,
And rowing on, unarrived, no matter how often he enter:
Like a big ship pushing her bowsprit over the little ships
Then swerving and steering afresh
And never, never arriving at journey's end, at the rear of the female ships.

Yellow eyes incomprehensible with thin slits
To round-eyed us.

Yet if you had whorled horns of bronze in a frontal dark wall
At the end of a back-bone ridge, like a straight *sierra roqueña*,
And nerves urging forward to the wall, you'd have eyes like his,
Especially if, being given a needle's eye of egress elsewhere
You tried to look back to it, and couldn't.

Sometimes he turns with a start, to fight, to challenge, to suddenly butt.
And then you see the God that he is, in a cloud of black hair
And storm-lightning-slitted eye.
Splendidly planting his feet, one rocky foot striking the ground with
       a sudden rock-hammer announcement.

I am here!
And suddenly lowering his head, the whorls of bone and of horn
Slowly revolving towards unexploded explosion,
As from the stem of his bristling, lightning-conductor tail
In a rush up the shrieking duct of his vertebral way
Runs a rage drawn in from the other divinely through him
Towards a shock and a crash and a smiting of horns ahead.

That is a grand old lust of his, to gather the great
Rage of the sullen-stagnating atmosphere of goats
And bring it hurtling to a head, with crash of horns against the horns
Of the opposite enemy goat,
Thus hammering the mettle of goats into proof, and smiting out
The godhead of goats from the shock.
Things of iron are beaten on the anvil,
And he-goat is anvil to he-goat, and hammer to he-goat
In the business of beating the mettle of goats to a godhead.

But they've taken his enemy from him
And left him only his libidinousness,
His nostrils turning back, to sniff at even himself
And his slitted eyes seeking the needle's eye,
His own, unthreaded, forever.

So it is, when they take the enemy from us,
And we can't fight.

He is not fatherly, like the bull, massive Providence of hot blood;
The goat is an egoist, aware of himself, devilish aware of himself,
And full of malice prepense, and overweening, determined to stand
        on the highest peak
Like the devil, and look on the world as his own.

And as for love:
With a needle of long red flint he stabs in the dark
At the living rock he is up against;
While she with her goaty mouth stands smiling the while as he strikes,
        since sure
He will never *quite* strike home, on the target-quick, for her quick
Is just beyond range of the arrow he shoots
From his leap at the zenith in her, so it falls just short of the mark, far
        enough.
It is over before it is finished.
She, smiling with goaty munch-mouth, Mona Lisa, arranges it so.

Orgasm after orgasm after orgasm
And he smells so rank and his nose goes back,

And never an enemy brow-metalled to thresh it out with in the open
        field;
Never a mountain peak, to be king of the castle.
Only those eternal females to overleap and surpass, and never succeed.

The involved voluptuousness of the soft-footed cat
Who is like a fur folding a fur,
The cat who laps blood, and knows
The soft welling of blood invincible even beyond bone or metal of bone.

The soft, the secret, the unfathomable blood
The cat has lapped
And known it subtler than frisson-shaken nerves,
Stronger than multiplicity of bone on bone
And darker than even the arrows of violentest will
Can pierce, for that is where will gives out, like a sinking stone that
        can sink no further.

But he-goat,
Black procreant male of the selfish will and libidinous desire,
God in black cloud with curving horns of bronze,
Find an enemy. Egoist, and clash the cymbals in face-to-face defiance,
And let the lightning out of your smothered dusk.

Forget the female herd for a bit,
And fight to be boss of the world.

Fight, old Satan with a selfish will, fight for your selfish will;
Fight to be the devil on the tip of the peak
Overlooking the world for his own.

But bah, how can he, poor domesticated beast!

Taormina

She Goat

Goats go past the back of the house like dry leaves in the dawn,
And up the hill like a river, if you watch.

At dusk they patter back like a bough being dragged on the ground,
Raising dusk and acridity of goats, and bleating.

Our old goat we tie up at night in the shed at the back of the broken
      Greek tomb in the garden,
And when the herd goes by at dawn she begins to bleat for me to
      come down and untie her.

Merr-err-err! Merr-er-errr! Mer! Me!
—*Wait, wait a bit, I'll come when I've lit the fire.*
Merrr!
—*Exactly.*
Mé! Mer! Merrrrrrr!!!
—*Tace, tu, crapa, bestia!*
Merr-ererrr-ererrrr! Merrrr!

She is such an alert listener, with her ears wide, to know am I coming!
Such a canny listener, from a distance, looking upwards, lending first
      one ear, then another.

There she is, perched on her manger, looking over the boards into the
      day
Like a belle at her window.
And immediately she sees me she blinks, stares, doesn't know me,
      turns her head and ignores me vulgarly with a wooden blank
      on her face.

What do I care for her, the ugly female, standing up there with her
      long tangled sides like an old rug thrown over a fence.
But she puts her nose down shrewdly enough when the knot is untied,
And jumps staccato to earth, a sharp, dry jump, still ignoring me,
Pretending to look round the stall.

Come on, you, crapa! I'm not your servant!

She turns her head away with an obtuse, female sort of deafness, bête.
And then invariably she crouches her rear and makes water.
That being her way of answer, if I speak to her.—Self-conscious!
Le bestie non parlano, poverine!

She was bought at Giardini fair, on the sands, for six hundred lire.

An obstinate old witch, almost jerking the rope from my hands to eat
      the acanthus, or bite at the almond buds, and make me wait.
Yet the moment I hate her she trips mild and smug like a woman
      going to mass.
The moment I really detest her.

Queer it is, suddenly, in the garden
To catch sight of her standing like some huge, ghoulish grey bird in
      the air, on the bough of the leaning almond-tree,
Straight as a board on the bough, looking down like some hairy horrid
      God the Father in a William Blake imagination.
Come down, crapa, out of that almond tree!

Instead of which she strangely rears on her perch in the air, vast beast.
And strangely paws the air, delicate,
And reaches her black-striped face up like a snake, far up,
Subtly, to the twigs overhead, far up, vast beast,
And snaps them sharp, with a little twist of her anaconda head;
All her great hairy-shaggy belly open against the morning.

At seasons she curls back her tail like a green leaf in the fire,
Or like a lifted hand, hailing at her wrong end.
And having exposed the pink place of her nakedness, fixedly.
She trots on blithe toes,
And if you look at her, she looks back with a cold, sardonic stare.
Sardonic, sardonyx, rock of cold fire.
See me? She says, *That's me!*

That's her.

Then she leaps the rocks like a quick rock,
Her back-bone sharp as a rock,

Sheer will.
Along which ridge of libidinous magnetism
Defiant, curling the leaf of her tail as if she were curling her lip
          behind her at all life,
Libidinous desire runs back and forth, asserting itself in that little
          lifted bare hand.

Yet she has such adorable spurty kids, like spurts of black ink.
And in a month again is as if she had never had them.

And when the billy goat mounts her
She is brittle as brimstone.
While his slitted eyes squint back to the roots of his ears.

Taormina

Elephant

You go down shade to the river, where naked men sit on flat brown
        rocks, to watch the ferry, in the sun;
And you cross the ferry with the naked people, go up the tropical lane
Through the palm-trees and past hollow paddy-fields where naked
        men are threshing rice
And the monolithic water-buffaloes, like old, muddy stones with hair
        on them, are being idle;
And through the shadow of bread-fruit trees, with their dark green,
        glossy, fanged leaves
Very handsome, and some pure yellow fanged leaves;
Out into the open, where the path runs on the top of a dyke between
        paddy-fields:
And there, of course, you meet a huge and mud-grey elephant
        advancing his frontal bone, his trunk curled round a log of
        wood:
So you step down the bank, to make way.

Shuffle, shuffle, and his little wicked eye has seen you as he advances
        above you,
The slow beast curiously spreading his round feet for the dust.
And the slim naked man slips down, and the beast deposits the lump
        of wood, carefully.
The keeper hooks the vast knee, the creature salaams.

White man, you are saluted.
Pay a few cents.

But the best is the Pera-hera, at midnight, under the tropical stars,
With a pale little wisp of a Prince of Wales, diffident, up in a small
        pagoda on the temple side
And white people in evening dress buzzing and crowding the stand
        upon the grass below and opposite:
And at last the Pera-hera procession, flambeaux aloft in the tropical
        night, of blazing cocoa-nut,
Naked dark men beneath,
And the huge frontal of three great elephants stepping forth to the
        tom-tom's beat, in the torch-light,

Slowly sailing in gorgeous apparel through the flame-light, in front
   of a towering, grimacing white image of wood.

The elephant bells striking slow, tong-tong, tong-tong,
To music and queer chanting:
Enormous shadow-processions filing on in the flare of fire
In the fume of cocoa-nut oil, in the sweating tropical night,
In the noise of the tom-toms and singers;
Elephants after elephants curl their trunks, vast shadows, and some
   cry out
As they approach and salaam, under the dripping fire of the torches
That pale fragment of a Prince up there, whose motto is *Ich dien*.

Pale, dispirited Prince, with his chin on his hands, his nerves tired out,
Watching and hardly seeing the trunk-curl approach and clumsy, knee-
   lifting salaam
Of the hugest, oldest of beasts in the night and the fire-flare below.
He is royalty, pale and dejected fragment up aloft.
And down below huge homage of shadowy beasts; barefoot and trunk
   lipped in the night.

Chieftains, three of them abreast, on foot
Strut like peg-tops, wound around with hundreds of yards of fine linen.
They glimmer with tissue of gold, and golden threads on a jacket of velvet,
And their faces are dark, and fat, and important.

They are royalty, dark-faced royalty, showing the conscious whites of
   their eyes
And stepping in homage, stubborn, to that nervous pale lad up there.

More elephants, tong, tong-tong, loom up,
Huge, more tassels swinging, more dripping fire of new cocoa-nut
   cressets
High, high flambeaux, smoking of the east;
And scarlet hot embers of torches knocked out of the sockets among
   bare feet of elephants and men on the path in the dark.
And devil dancers luminous with sweat, dancing on to the shudder of
   drums,

Tom-toms, weird music of the devil, voices of men from the jungle
     singing;
Endless, under the Prince.

Towards the tail of the everlasting procession
In the long hot night, mere dancers from insignificant villages,
And smaller, more frightened elephants.
Men-peasants from jungle villages dancing and running with sweat
     and laughing,
Naked dark men with ornaments on, on their naked arms and their
     naked breasts, the grooved loins
Gleaming like metal with running sweat as they suddenly turn, feet
     apart,
And dance, and dance, forever dance, with breath half sobbing in
     dark, sweat-shining breasts,
And lustrous great tropical eyes unveiled now, gleaming a kind of laugh,
A naked, gleaming dark laugh, like a secret out in the dark,
And flare of a tropical energy, tireless, afire in the dark, slim limbs and
     breasts,
Perpetual, fire-laughing motion, among the slow shuffle
Of elephants,
The hot dark blood of itself a-laughing, wet, half-devilish, men all
     motion
Approaching under that small pavilion, and tropical eyes dilated look up
Inevitably look up
To the Prince
To that tired remnant of royalty up there
Whose motto is *Ich dien*.

As if the homage of the kindled blood of the east
Went up in wavelets to him, from the breasts and eyes of jungle torch-
     men,
And he couldn't take it.

What would they do, those jungle men running with sweat, with the
     strange dark laugh in their eyes, glancing up,
And the sparse-haired elephants slowly following,
If they knew that his motto was *Ich dien*?
And that he meant it.

They begin to understand
The rickshaw boys begin to understand
And then the devil comes into their faces,
But a different sort, a cold, rebellious, jeering devil.

In elephants and the east are two devils, in all men maybe.
The mystery of the dark mountain of blood, reeking in homage, in
        lust, in rage,
And passive with everlasting patience,
Then the little, cunning pig-devil of the elephant's lurking eyes, the
        unbeliever.

We dodged, when the Pera-hera was finished, under the hanging,
        hairy pigs' tails
And the flat, flaccid mountains of the elephants' standing haunches.
Vast-blooded beasts,
Myself so little dodging rather scared against the eternal wrinkled
        pillars of their legs, as they were being dismantled;
Then I knew they were dejected, having come to hear the repeated
Royal summons: *Dient Ihr!*
Serve!
Serve, vast mountainous blood, in submission and splendour, serve royalty.
Instead of which, the silent, fatal emission from that pale, shattered
        boy up there:
Ich dien.

That's why the night fell in frustration.
That's why, as the elephants ponderously, with unseeming swiftness,
        galloped uphill in the night, going back to the jungle villages,
As the elephant bells sounded tong-tong-tong, bell of the temple of
        blood in the night, swift-striking,
And the crowd like a field of rice in the dark gave way like liquid to
        the dark
Looming gallop of the beasts,
It was as if the great bare bulks of elephants in the obscure light went
        over the hill-brow swiftly, with their tails between their legs,
        in haste to get away,
Their bells sounding frustrate and sinister.

And all the dark-faced, cotton-wrapped people, more numerous and
　　　　whispering than grains of rice in a rice-field at night,
All the dark-faced, cotton-wrapped people, a countless host on the
　　　　shores of the lake, like thick wild rice by the water's edge,
Waiting for the fireworks of the after-show,
As the rockets went up, and the glare passed over countless faces,
　　　　dark as black rice growing,
Showing a glint of teeth, and glancing tropical eyes aroused in the night,
There was the faintest twist of mockery in every face, across the hiss
　　　　of wonders as the rocket burst
High, high up, in flakes, shimmering flakes of blue fire, above the
　　　　palm-trees of the islet in the lake,
O faces upturned to the glare, O tropical wonder, wonder, a miracle
　　　　in heaven!
And the shadow of a jeer, of underneath disappointment, as the rocket-
　　　　coruscation died, and shadow was the same as before.

They were foiled, the myriad whispering dark-faced cotton-wrapped
　　　　people.
They had come to see royalty,
To bow before royalty, in the land of elephants, bow deep, bow deep.
Bow deep, for it's good us a draught of cool water to bow very, very
　　　　low to the royal.

And all there was to bow to, a weary, diffident boy whose motto is
　　　　Ich dien.
I serve! I serve! in all the weary iron of his mien—'Tis I who serve!
Drudge to the public.

I wish they had given the three feathers to me;
That I had been he in the pavilion, as in a pepper-box aloft and alone
To stand and hold feathers, three feathers above the world,
And say to them: *Dient Ihr! Dient!*
Omnes, vos omnes, servite.
Serve me, I am meet to be served.
Being royal of the gods.

And to the elephants:
First great beasts of the earth

A prince has come back to you,
Blood-mountains.
Crook the knee and be glad.

Kandy

Kangaroo

In the northern hemisphere
Life seems to leap at the air, or skim under the wind
Like stags on rocky ground, or pawing horses, or springy scut-tailed
      rabbits.

Or else rush horizontal to charge at the sky's horizon,
Like bulls or bisons or wild pigs.

Or slip like water slippery towards its ends,
As foxes, stoats, and wolves, and prairie dogs.

Only mice, and moles, and rats, and badgers, and beavers, and
      perhaps bears
Seem belly-plumbed to the earth's mid-navel.
Or frogs that when they leap come flop, and flop to the centre of the
      earth.

But the yellow antipodal Kangaroo, when she sits up,
Who can unseat her, like a liquid drop that is heavy, and just touches
      earth.

The downward drip.
The down-urge.
So much denser than cold-blooded frogs.

Delicate mother Kangaroo
Sitting up there rabbit-wise, but huge, plumb-weighted,
And lifting her beautiful slender face, oh! so much more gently and
      finely lined than a rabbit's, or than a hare's,
Lifting her face to nibble at a round white peppermint drop, which
      she loves, sensitive mother Kangaroo.

Her sensitive, long, pure-bred face.
Her full antipodal eyes, so dark,
So big and quiet and remote, having watched so many empty dawns
      in silent Australia.

Her little loose hands, and drooping Victorian shoulders.
And then her great weight below the waist, her vast pale belly
With a thin young yellow little paw hanging out, and straggle of a
        long thin ear, like ribbon,
Like a funny trimming to the middle of her belly, thin little dangle
        of an immature paw, and one thin ear.

Her belly, her big haunches
And in addition, the great muscular python-stretch of her tail.

There, she shan't have any more peppermint drops.
So she wistfully, sensitively sniffs the air, and then turns, goes off in
        slow sad leaps

On the long flat skis of her legs,
Steered and propelled by that steel-strong snake of a tail.

Stops again, half turns, inquisitive to look back.
While something stirs quickly in her belly, and a lean little face comes
        out, as from a window,
Peaked and a bit dismayed,
Only to disappear again quickly away from the sight of the world, to
        snuggle down in the warmth,
Leaving the trail of a different paw hanging out.

Still she watches with eternal, cocked wistfulness!
How full her eyes are, like the full, fathomless, shining eyes of an
        Australian black-boy
Who has been lost so many centuries on the margins of existence!

She watches with insatiable wistfulness.
Untold centuries of watching for something to come,
For a new signal from life, in that silent lost land of the South.

Where nothing bites but insects and snakes and the sun, small life.
Where no bull roared, no cow ever lowed, no stag cried, no leopard
        screeched, no lion coughed, no dog barked,
But all was silent save for parrots occasionally, in the haunted blue bush.

Wistfully watching, with wonderful liquid eyes.
And all her weight, all her blood, dripping sack-wise down towards
      the earth's centre,
And the live little one taking in its paw at the door of her belly.

Leap then, and come down on the line that draws to the earth's deep,
      heavy centre.

Sydney

Bibbles

Little black dog in New Mexico,
Little black snub-nosed bitch with a shoved-out jaw
And a wrinkled reproachful look;
Little black female pup, sort of French bull, they say,
With bits of brindle coming through, like rust, to show you're not pure;
Not pure, Bibbles,
Bubsey, bat-eared dog;
Not black enough!

First live thing I've "owned" since the lop-eared rabbits when I was a lad,
And those over-prolific white mice, and Adolf, and Rex whom I didn't
        own.
And even now, Bibbles, little Ma'am, it's you who appropriated me,
        not I you.
As Benjamin Franklin appropriated Providence to his purposes.

Oh Bibbles, black little bitch
I'd never have let you appropriate me, had I known.
I never dreamed, till now, of the awful time the Lord must have,
        "owning" humanity,
Especially democratic live-by-love humanity.

Oh Bibbles, oh Pips, oh Pipsey
You little black love-bird!
Don't you love *everybody*!
Just everybody.
You love 'em all.
Believe in the One Identity, don't you,
You little Walt-Whitmanesque bitch?

First time I lost you in Taos plaza,
And found you after endless chasing,
Came upon you prancing round the corner in exuberant, bibbling
        affection
After the black-green skirts of a yellow-green old Mexican woman
Who hated you, and kept looking round at you and cursing you in a
        mutter,

156

While you pranced and bounced with love of her, you indiscriminating
        animal,
All your wrinkled *miserere* Chinese black little face beaming
And your black little body bouncing and wriggling
With indiscriminate love, Bibbles;
I had a moment's pure detestation of you.

As I rushed like an idiot round the corner after you
Yelling: *Pips! Pips! Bibbles!*

I've had moments of hatred of you since,
Loving everybody!
"To you, whoever you are, with endless embrace!"—
That's you, Pipsey,
With your imbecile bit of a tail in a love-flutter.
You omnipip.

Not that you're merely a softy, oh dear me no.
You know which side your bread is buttered.
You don't care a rap for anybody.
But you love lying warm between warm human thighs, indiscriminate,
And you love to make somebody love you, indiscriminate,
You love to lap up affection, to wallow in it,
And then turn tail to the next comer, for a new dollop.

And start prancing and licking and cuddling again, indiscriminate.

Oh yes, I know your little game.

Yet you're so nice,
So quick, like a little black dragon.
So fierce, when the coyotes howl, barking like a whole little lion, and
        rumbling,
And starting forward in the dusk, with your little black fur all
        bristling like plush
Against those coyotes, who would swallow you like an oyster.

And in the morning, when the bedroom door is opened,
Rushing in like a little black whirlwind, leaping straight as an arrow
        on the bed at the pillow

And turning the day suddenly into a black tornado of *joie de vivre*,
        Chinese dragon.

So funny
Lobbing wildly through deep snow like a rabbit,
Hurtling like a black ball through the snow,
Champing it, tossing a mouthful,
Little black spot in the landscape!

So absurd
Pelting behind on the dusty trail when the horse sets off home at a
        gallop:
Left in the dust behind like a dust-ball tearing along
Coming up on fierce little legs, tearing fast to catch up, a real little
        dust-pig, ears almost blown away,
And black eyes bulging bright in a dust-mask
Chinese-dragon-wrinkled, with a pink mouth grinning, under jaw
        shoved out
And white teeth showing in your dragon-grin as you race, you split-face.
Like a trundling projectile swiftly whirling up,
Cocking your eyes at me as you come alongside, to see if I'm I on the
        horse,
And panting with that split grin,
All your game little body dust-smooth like a little pig, poor Pips.

Plenty of game old spirit in you, Bibbles.
Plenty of game old spunk, little bitch.

How you hate being brushed with the boot-brush, to brush all that
        dust out of your wrinkled face,
Don't you?
How you hate being made to look undignified. Ma'am;
How you hate being laughed at. Miss Superb!

Blackberry face!

Plenty of conceit in you.
Unblemished belief in your own perfection
And utter lovableness, you ugly-mug;

Chinese puzzle-face,
Wrinkled underhung physiog that looks as if it had done with
        everything,
Through with everything.

Instead of which you sit there and roll your head like a canary
And show a tiny bunch of white teeth in your underhung blackness,
Self-conscious little bitch,
Aiming again at being loved.

Let the merest scallywag come to the door and you leap your very
        dearest-love at him,
As if now, at last, here was the one you *finally* loved,
Finally loved;
And even the dirtiest scallywag is taken in,
Thinking: *This dog sure has taken a fancy to me.*

You miserable little bitch of love-tricks,
I know your game.

Me or the Mexican who comes to chop wood
All the same,
All humanity is jam to you.

Everybody so dear, and yourself so ultra-beloved
That you have to run out at last and eat filth,
Gobble up filth, you horror, swallow utter abomination and fresh-
        dropped dung.

You stinker.
You worse than a carrion-crow.
Reeking dung-mouth.
You love-bird.

Reject nothing, sings Walt Whitman.
So you, you go out at last and eat the unmentionable,
In your appetite for affection.

And then you run in to vomit it in my house!
I get my love back.

And I have to clean up after you, filth which even blind Nature rejects
From the pit of your stomach;
But you, you snout-face, you reject nothing, you merge so much in love
You must eat even that.

Then when I dust you a bit with a juniper twig
You run straight away to live with somebody else,
Fawn before them, and love them as if they were the ones you had
      really loved all along.
And they're taken in.
They feel quite tender over you, till you play the same trick on them,
      dirty bitch.

Fidelity! Loyalty! Attachment!
Oh, these are abstractions to your nasty little belly.
You must always be a-waggle with LOVE.
Such a waggle of love you can hardly distinguish one human from
      another.

You love one after another, on one condition, that each one loves you
      most.
Democratic little bull-bitch, dirt-eating little swine.

But now, my lass, you've got your Nemesis on your track,
Now you've come sex-alive, and the great ranch-dogs are all after you.
They're after what they can get, and don't you turn tail!
You loved 'em all so much before, didn't you, loved 'em indiscriminate.
You don't love 'em now.
They want something of you, so you squeak and come pelting indoors.

Come pelting to me, now the other folk have found you out, and the
      dogs are after you.
Oh yes, you're found out. I heard them kick you out of the ranch house.
Get out, you little, soft fool!!

And didn't you turn your eyes up at me then?
And didn't you cringe on the floor like any inkspot!
And crawl away like a black snail!
And doesn't everybody loathe you then!
And aren't your feelings violated, you high bred little love-bitch!

160

For you're sensitive,
In many ways very finely bred.
But bred in conceit that the world is all for love
Of you, my bitch: till you get so far you eat filth.
Fool, in spite of your pretty ways, and quaint, know all, wrinkled old
        aunty's face.

So now, what with great Airedale dogs,
And a kick or two,
And a few vomiting bouts,
And a juniper switch,
You look at me for discrimination, don't you?
Look up at me with misgiving in your bulging eyes,
And fear in the smoky whites of your eyes, you nigger;
And you're puzzled,
You think you'd better mind your Ps and Qs for a bit,
Your sensitive love-pride being all hurt.

All right, my little bitch.
You learn loyalty rather than loving,
And I'll protect you.

Lobo

Mountain Lion

Climbing through the January snow, into the Lobo canyon
Dark grow the spruce-trees, blue is the balsam, water sounds still
        unfrozen, and the trail is still evident.

Men!
Two men!
Men! The only animal in the world to fear!

They hesitate.
We hesitate.
They have a gun.
We have no gun.

Then we all advance, to meet.

Two Mexicans, strangers, emerging out of the dark and snow and
        inwardness of the Lobo valley.
What are they doing here on this vanishing trail?

What is he carrying?
Something yellow.
A deer?

Que tiene, amigo?
León—

He smiles, foolishly, as if he were caught doing wrong.
And we smile, foolishly, as if we didn't know.
He is quite gentle and dark-faced.

It is a mountain lion,
A long, long slim cat, yellow like a lioness.
Dead.

He trapped her this morning, he says, smiling foolishly.

Lift up her face,
Her round, bright face, bright as frost.
Her round, fine-fashioned head, with two dead ears;
And stripes in the brilliant frost of her face, sharp, fine dark rays,
Dark, keen, fine rays in the brilliant frost of her face.
Beautiful dead eyes.

Hermoso es!

They go out towards the open;
We go on into the gloom of Lobo.
And above the trees I found her lair,
A hole in the blood-orange brilliant rocks that stick up, a little cave.
And bones, and twigs, and a perilous ascent.

So, she will never leap up that way again, with the yellow flash of a
      mountain lion's long shoot!
And her bright striped frost face will never watch any more, out of
      the shadow of the cave in the blood-orange rock,
Above the trees of the Lobo dark valley-mouth!

Instead, I look out.
And out to the dim of the desert, like a dream, never real;
To the snow of the Sangre de Cristo mountains, the ice of the
      mountains of Picoris,
And near across at the opposite steep of snow, green trees motionless
      standing in snow, like a Christmas toy.

And I think in this empty world there was room for me, and a
      mountain lion.
And I think in the world beyond, how easily we might spare a
      million or two of humans
And never miss them.
Yet what a gap in the world, the missing white frost face of that slim
      yellow mountain lion!

Lobo

The Red Wolf

Over the heart of the west, the Taos desert
Circles an eagle,
And it's dark between me and him.

The sun, as he waits a moment, huge and liquid
Standing without feet on the rim of the far-off mesa
Says: *Look for a last long time then! Look! Look well! I am going.*
So he pauses and is beholden, and straightway is gone.

And the Indian, in a white sheet
Wrapped to the eyes, the sheet bound close on his brows,
Stands saying: *See, I'm invisible!*
Behold how you cant behold me!
The invisible in its shroud!

Now that the sun has gone, and the aspen leaves
And the cotton-wood leaves are fallen, as good as fallen,
And the ponies are in corral,
And it's night.

Why, more has gone than all these;
And something has come.
A red wolf stands on the shadow's dark red rim.

Day has gone to dust on the sage-grey desert
Like a white Christus fallen to dust from a cross;
To dust, to ash, on the twilit floor of the desert.

And a black crucifix like a dead tree spreading wings;
Maybe a black eagle with its wings out
Left lonely in the night
In a sort of worship.

And coming down upon us, out of the dark concave
Of the eagle's wings,
And the coffin-like slit where the Indian's eyes are,
And the absence of cotton-wood leaves, or of aspen,

Even the absence of dark-crossed donkeys:
Come tall old demons, smiling
The Indian smile,
Saying: *How do you do, you pale-face?*

I am very well, old demon.
How are you?

Call me Harry if you will,
Call me Old Harry says he.
Or the abbreviation of Nicolas,
Nick. Old Nick, maybe.

Well, you're a dark old demon,
And I'm a pale-face like a homeless dog
That has followed the sun from the dawn through the east
Trotting east and east and east till the sun himself went home,
And left me homeless here in the dark at your door.
How do you think we'll get on,
Old demon, you and I?

You and I, you pale-face,
Pale-face you and I
Don't get on.

Mightn't we try?

Where's your God, you white one?
Where's your white God?

He fell to dust as the twilight fell,
Was fume as I trod
The last step out of the east.

Then you're a lost white dog of a pale-face,
And the day's now dead . . .

Touch me carefully, old father,
My beard is red.

Thin red wolf of a pale-face,
Thin red wolf, go home.

I have no home, old father,
That's why I come.

We take no hungry stray from the pale-face . . .

Father, you are not asked.
I am come. I am here. The red-dawn-wolf
Sniffs round your place.
Lifts up his voice and howls to the walls of the pueblo,
Announcing he's here.

The dogs of the dark pueblo
Have long fangs . . .

Has the red wolf trotted east and east and east
From the far, far other end of the day
To fear a few fangs?

Across the pueblo river
That dark old demon and I
Thus say a few words to each other

And wolf, he calls me, and red.
I call him no names.
He says, however, he is Star-Road.
I say, he can go back the same gait.

As for me . . .
Since I trotted at the tail of the sun as far as ever the creature
went west,
And lost him here,
I'm going to sit down on my tail right here
And wait for him to come back with a new story.
I'm the red wolf, says the dark old father.
All right, the red dawn wolf I am.

Taos

166

GHOSTS

"And as the dog with its nostrils tracking out the fragments of the beasts' limbs, and the breath from their feet that they leave in the soft grass, runs upon a path that is pathless to men, so does the soul follow the trail of the dead, across great spaces. For the journey is a far one, to sleep and a forgetting, and often the dead look back, and linger, for now they realise all that is lost. Then the living soul comes up with them, and great is the pain of greeting, and deadly the parting again. For oh, the dead are disconsolate, since even death can never make up for some mistakes."

Men in New Mexico

Mountains blanket-wrapped
Round a white hearth of desert—

While the sun goes round
And round and round the desert,
The mountains never get up and walk about.
They can't, they can't wake.

They camped and went to sleep
In the last twilight
Of Indian gods;
And they can't wake.

Indians dance and run and stamp—
No good.
White men make gold-mines and the mountains unmake them
In their sleep.

The Indians laugh in their sleep
From fear,
Like a man when he sleeps and his sleep is over, and he can't wake up,
And he lies like a log and screams and his scream is silent
Because his body can't wake up;
So he laughs from fear, pure fear, in the grip of the sleep.

A dark membrane over the will, holding a man down
Even when the mind has flickered awake;
A membrane of sleep, like a black blanket.

We walk in our sleep, in this land,
Somnambulist wide-eyed afraid.

We scream for someone to wake us
And our scream is soundless in the paralysis of sleep.
And we know it.

The Penitentes lash themselves till they run with blood
In their efforts to come awake for one moment;
To tear the membrane of this sleep . . .
No good.

The Indians thought the white man would awake them . . .
And instead, the white men scramble asleep in the mountains,
And ride on horseback asleep forever through the desert,
And shoot one another, amazed and mad with somnambulism,
Thinking death will awaken something . . .
No good.

Born with a caul,
A black membrane over the face,
And unable to tear it,
Though the mind is awake.

Mountains blanket-wrapped
Round the ash-white hearth of the desert;
And though the sun leaps like a thing unleashed in the sky
They can't get up, they are under the blanket.

Taos

Autumn at Taos

Over the rounded sides of the Rockies, the aspens of autumn,
The aspens of autumn,
Like yellow hair of a tigress brindled with pine.

Down on my hearth-rug of desert, sage of the mesa,
An ash-grey pelt
Of wolf all hairy and level, a wolf's wild pelt.

Trot-trot to the mottled foot-hills, cedar-mottled and piñon;
Did you ever see an otter?
Silvery-sided, fish-fanged, fierce-faced whiskered, mottled.

When I trot my little pony through the aspen-trees of the canyon,
Behold me trotting at ease betwixt the slopes of the golden
Great and glistening-feathered legs of the hawk of Horus;
The golden hawk of Horus
Astride above me.

But under the pines
I go slowly
As under the hairy belly of a great black bear.

Glad to emerge and look back
On the yellow, pointed aspen-trees laid one on another like feathers,
Feather over feather on the breast of the great and golden
Hawk as I say of Horus.

Pleased to be out in the sage and the pine fish-dotted foothills,
Past the otter's whiskers,
On to the fur of the wolf-pelt that strews the plain.

And then to look back to the rounded sides of the squatting Rockies,
Tigress brindled with aspen
Jaguar-splashed, puma-yellow, leopard-livid slopes of America.

Make big eyes, little pony
At all these skins of wild beasts;
They won't hurt you.

Fangs and claws and talons and beaks and hawk-eyes
Are nerveless just now.
So be easy.

Taos

Note: Line 3 *pine.* The *Collected Poems* has "pines"; the first UK edition of *Birds, Beasts and Flowers* has "pins", which is evidently a typographical error. We have here preferred the reading from the US edition of this book.

Spirits Summoned West

England seems full of graves to me,
Full of graves.

Women I loved and cherished, like my mother;
Yet I had to tell them to die.

England seems covered with graves to me,
Women's graves.

Women who were gentle
And who loved me
And whom I loved
And told to die.

Women with the beautiful eyes of the old days,
Belief in love, and sorrow of such belief.
"Hush, my love, then, hush.
Hush, and die, my dear!"

Women of the older generation, who knew
The full doom of loving and not being able to take back.
Who understood at last what it was to be told to die.

Now that the graves are made, and covered;
Now that in England pansies and such-like grow on the graves of
        women;
Now that in England is silence, where before was a moving of soft-
        skirted women,
Women with eyes that were gentle in olden belief in love;
Now then that all their yearning is hushed, and covered over with earth.

England seems like one grave to me.

And I, I sit on this high American desert
With dark-wrapped Rocky Mountains motionless squatting around
        in a ring,
Remembering I told them to die, to sink into the grave in England,
The gentle-kneed women.

So now I whisper: *Come away,*
Come away from the place of graves, come west,
Women,
Women whom I loved and told to die.

Come back to me now,
Now the divided yearning is over;
Now you are husbandless indeed, no more husband to cherish like a child
And wrestle with for the prize of perfect love.
No more children to launch in a world you mistrust.
Now you need know in part
No longer, or carry the burden of a man on your heart,
Or the burden of Man writ large.

Now you are disemburdened of Man and a man
Come back to me.
Now you are free of the toils of a would-be-perfect love
Come to me and be still.

Come back then, you who were wives and mothers
And always virgins
Overlooked.

Come back then, mother, my love, whom I told to die.
It was only I who saw the virgin you
That had no home.

The overlooked virgin,
My love.

You overlooked her too.

Now that the grave is made of mother and wife,
Now that the grave is made and lidded over with turf.

Come, delicate, overlooked virgin, come back to me
And be still,
Be glad.

I didn't tell you to die, for nothing.
I wanted the virgin you to be home at last
In my heart.

Inside my innermost heart,
Where the virgin in woman comes home to a man.

The homeless virgin
Who never in all her life could find the way home
To that difficult innermost place in a man.

Now come west, come home,
Women I've loved for gentleness,
For the virginal you.
Find the way now that you never could find in life,
So I told you to die.

Virginal first and last
Is woman.
Now at this last, my love, my many a love,
You whom I loved for gentleness,
Come home to me.

They are many, and I loved them, shall always love them,
And they know it,
The virgins.
And my heart is glad to have them at last.

Now that the wife and mother and mistress is buried in earth,
In English earth,
Come home to me, my love, my loves, my many loves,
Come west to me.

For virgins are not exclusive of virgins
As wives are of wives;
And motherhood is jealous,
But in virginity jealousy does not enter.

Taos

The American Eagle

The dove of Liberty sat on an egg
And hatched another eagle.

But didn't disown the bird.

Down with all eagles! cooed the Dove.
And down all eagles began to flutter, reeling from their perches:
Eagles with two heads, eagles with one, presently eagles with none
Fell from the hooks and were dead.

Till the American Eagle was the only eagle left in the world.

Then it began to fidget, shifting from one leg to the other,
Trying to look like a pelican,
And plucking out of his plumage a few loose feathers to feather the
          nests of all
The new naked little republics come into the world.

But the feathers were, comparatively, a mere flea-bite.
And the bub-eagle that Liberty had hatched was growing a startling
          big bird
On the roof of the world;
A bit awkward, and with a funny squawk in his voice,
His mother Liberty trying always to teach him to coo
And him always ending with a yawp
Coo! Coo! Coo! Coo-ark! Coo-ark! Quark!! Quark!!
Yawp!!!

So he clears his throat, the young Cock-eagle!

Now if the lilies of France lick Solomon in all his glory;
And the leopard cannot change his spots;
Nor the British lion his appetite,
Neither can a young Cock-eagle sit simpering
With an olive-sprig in his mouth.

It's not his nature.

The big bird of the Amerindian being the eagle,
Red Men still stick themselves over with bits of his fluff,
And feel absolutely IT.

So better make up your mind, American Eagle,
Whether you're a sucking dove, *Roo — coo — ooo! Quark! Yawp!!*
Or a pelican
Handing out a few loose golden breast-feathers, at moulting time;
Or a sort of prosperity-gander
Fathering endless ten-dollar golden eggs.

Or whether it actually is an eagle you are,
With a Roman nose
And claws not made to shake hands with,
And a Me-Almighty eye.

The new Proud Republic
Based on the mystery of pride.
Overweening men, full of power of life, commanding a teeming
        obedience.

Eagle of the Rockies, bird of men that are masters,
Lifting the rabbit-blood of the myriads up into something splendid,
Leaving a few bones;
Opening great wings in the face of the sheep-faced ewe
Who is losing her lamb,
Drinking a little blood, and loosing another royalty unto the world.

Is that you, American Eagle?

Or are you the goose that lays the golden egg?
Which is just a stone to anyone asking for meat.
And are you going to go on for ever
Laying that golden egg,
That addled golden egg?

Lobo

CPSIA information can be obtained at www.ICGtesting.com
Printed in the USA
BVOW022214160412

287824BV00001B/58/P